Dare to Dream

A Small-town Kid's Journey to NASA

A Memoir by:

Dr. Jason K. Cornelius

Published by
Cornelius Unlimited LLC
Dallas, PA 18612

Copyright © 2024 Dr. Jason K. Cornelius
All rights reserved.

No part of this book may be reproduced, stored in a retrieval system, or transmitted in any form or by any means—electronic, mechanical, photocopying, recording, or otherwise—without the prior written permission of the publisher.

First Edition

ISBN 979-8-9919969-0-7
E-Book ISBN 979-8-9919969-1-4

This is a memoir based on the author's recollections of events, people, and places. Some names and identifying details have been changed to respect privacy. The author has made every effort to ensure accuracy; however, certain events may be subject to memory limitations and personal perspective.

Printed in the United States of America

All expressions, ideas, and opinions are my own and do not represent anyone else's, including that of my current, past, or future employers.

Graphic Designer: Emily Charron

DEDICATION

I come as one, but stand as 10,000. To all those I've met on my journey, thank you. You may not realize just how much our crossing paths has influenced my life for the better. I wish each of you all the best that life has to offer.

To my family and friends for always putting up with my crazy ideas.

To my mother, for being a rock in a stormy sea.

AUTHOR'S NOTE

The story in these pages is as true as I could recreate it from my memory, photographs, and journal entries. To enhance readability and respect the privacy of certain individuals, some characters have been combined or given different names, and a few events have been adapted with slight literary license. Though I've made these adjustments to improve the narrative flow, the essence of the experiences remains faithfully true to my journey.

All expressions, ideas, and opinions are my own and do not represent anyone else's, including that of my current, past, or future employers.

ACKNOWLEDGEMENTS

Writing this book has been a true labor of love. For years, I wanted to tell my story but hesitated, fearing what others might think. Over time, I've grown to care less about how my goals are perceived, though I still choose carefully when sharing big ideas. Writing your life story for others to see is, after all, no small undertaking.

When I first started this journey, I turned to my brother Ryan. His encouragement to explore my story through writing gave me the confidence to continue. His early feedback was instrumental in helping me transition from the technical style I was accustomed to at work into what I hope is an engaging and conversational narrative.

In addition to Ryan, several friends graciously reviewed the first draft. I am deeply grateful to Maysoor, Tove, Athena, and Dalton for their honest feedback and thoughtful suggestions, which shaped this manuscript for a broader audience. My heartfelt thanks also go to my family—my mother, father, brother, and sister—not only for their feedback but for being integral parts of the story itself.

Emily Charron, my graphic designer, deserves special recognition for her impeccable work on the book's artwork. She distilled 62,000 words into graphics capturing the essence of my journey. Her creativity, along with input from a handful of friends, elevated the book's visual appeal to something I am truly proud of.

To all the others who have supported, encouraged, and believed in me along the way—thank you. Whether through kind words, thoughtful advice, or simple gestures of faith in my journey, your contributions mean more than words can express. I continue to be a product of my circumstances and those around me, and I am grateful for each and every one of you. I hope you know who you are.

CONTENTS

1	An Astronaut's Gold Visor	15
2	Building Momentum	23
3	When Life Knocks You Down	33
4	Penn State – 1 of 5 Will Graduate	43
5	China – Scorpions on a Stick	53
6	Finding The Balance	67
7	Texas – Honey Butter Chicken Biscuits	77
8	The Hardest Semester of Your Life	87
9	NASA Interns – Roger Bannister	99
10	China and Texas Take 2 – Mr. Motivator	111
11	Diversifying Interests	125
12	NASA II – There are Always Flowers	137
13	Flying By The Seat of Your Pants	147
14	Winter Training in Russia	157
15	Oath of Office	173
	Reflections	180

EPIGRAPH

Matthew 7:7-8 (c. 80-90 AD)

"Ask, and it shall be given you;
seek, and ye shall find;
knock, and it shall be opened unto you:
for every one that asketh receiveth;
and he that seeketh findeth;
and to him that knocketh it shall be opened."

I came across this quote mid-way through a decade-long pursuit of a childhood dream: to work for NASA. That goal proved to be the adventure of a lifetime. Along the way, I encountered many doors that seemed closed, and some that slammed shut in my face.

At first, this quote felt overly optimistic to me. It painted a magical view of the world as if one could exercise their will on the outcomes of their life. But over time, I learned that this is precisely how the world works. My story is one of persistently knocking on doors to the future. Sometimes they opened, and sometimes I had to look for another door to try.

In the end, persistence, determination, resilience, and hard work were the keys that led me to what I was looking for.

PROLOGUE

My life has been full of times when someone told me what can't be done, or more specifically, what I couldn't do. My earliest memory of something like this was when my elementary school rejected my application to the gifted program that my older brother was practically invited into. At the time, it was easy for me to not care that much, the gifted program meant extra work and assignments anyway. Over the next several years, however, the lack of academic rigor offered by the normal curriculum in my small-town grade school led me to become quite a mischievous youngster.

What I hadn't appreciated until very recently, however, was the fire that the proclamation 'you can't do this' would light inside of me. In the seventh grade, a Wikipedia page changed my life and I decided to take matters into my own hands. I had no idea the roller coaster of an adventure I was about to embark on. Over the next 10 years, I would hear many more people tell me what I couldn't do:

"Yeah right! You'lll never make it to NASA."

"We regret to inform you that you weren't selected to be part of the Penn State Schreyer Honors College."

"HA! You can't get that scholarship, only the best students in the entire university have a shot at those."

"I am writing to let you know that unfortunately you were not selected as a Penn State finalist for the Astronaut Foundation Scholarship."

"Your commitment to applied research is perceived in some circles as a weakness."

"You're going to learn Russian? Good luck."

"We regret to inform you that we are unable to offer you admission to the Master of Science program in Aerospace Engineering."

This memoir tells the story of ten years of my life, starting from that day in the 7th grade that I decided to aim up in life. It's an account of what the human mind and spirit are capable of despite a myriad of people you look up to and respect telling you those things are unrealistic or out of reach for you. Still today, people tell me all the time what 'can' and 'cannot' be done. I have proven to myself the benefits of politely ignoring limitations others proclaim for your life, especially when their vision for your future is smaller than your own.

We each have one spin on the wheel of life, and in my opinion, you should make it the best one possible. If you've ever doubted the possibilities for your future, or wondered if the thoughts of others are right, then I invite you to read on and discover the story of a kid from a small railway town in Northeastern Pennsylvania who demanded life give him more than what others thought was possible. This is a story of a kid that pursued an alternate future even before the rest of the world, his family, his closest friends, **and at times even he** believed was possible.

When did I decide to write this book? The idea first came around 2017 and solidified in 2018 during my time in Russia. What do I want to tell the world? In principle, it's *my* story. When did I succeed, when did I fail, when did I become better, and when did I want to give up and shut it all down. Although my story may be interesting to those that know me personally, I hope a much broader audience benefits from the lessons and conclusions I've drawn from my journey.

The overarching theme of this story is that we each get to choose our future. No matter what outcome you choose for your life, there will be ups and downs along the way. **Once you've set your mind to something, the only thing that can truly stop you, is you.** And if there are going to be highs and lows no matter what future you choose, you might as well choose an exciting one. I decided I would become an aerospace engineer working at NASA someday. It was a long and difficult road. And in the beginning, very few people believed I could actually do it.

On this journey to discover myself, I learned some really interesting things as I tried to make sense of the world around me. I met thousands of people as I learned their perspectives, their wisdom, and sometimes even their language.

So what were the most important discoveries of this journey that I'd like to share with you? Which experiences have rocked the foundation of who I am, to develop me into someone better on the other side? These are the questions we'll explore in the pages of this book.

"Sometimes life hits you in the head with a brick. Don't lose faith." — Steve Jobs

In the summer of 2018 I found myself in a whirlwind adventure in Silicon Valley, California. It was my third student internship at the NASA Ames Research Center in the Rotorcraft Aeromechanics Office, which focuses on both terrestrial and extra-terrestrial rotary-wing (helicopter) engineering. Just weeks earlier, I returned to the United States from a four month intensive training program in St. Petersburg, Russia. To put the cherry on top, I would be starting my Masters degree in aerospace engineering at Penn State fully paid for by the National Science Foundation (NSF) to design a space helicopter going to Saturn's moon, Titan. I was floating on top of the world and felt like I was unstoppable, for a brief moment of time.

I suppose I was too comfortable and the universe decided to send me a message bringing me back down to reality. Mid-way through my NASA internship, Penn State gave me a phone call, "You are not allowed to both work at NASA and be sponsored by NSF for graduate school." Over the course of a thirty second phone call, my dream came crashing down around me. I wondered to myself, "Would I give up working for NASA to continue working towards my PhD that I was so set on?" "Could I even bring myself to do that?" Life had no doubt hit me in the head with a brick.

I took the 100 foot walk down to my supervisor's office. And with each step my brain was spinning further out of control. Bill is the longest standing branch manager in all NASA with 40 years of service. My mind and heart were racing, and his years in management enabled him to instantly recognize the seriousness of the situation. He immediately set aside whatever he had been working on. "Come on in, sit down," he suggested.

I walked him through the phone call, and like two rationale engineers, we tried working through the problem. The NSF fellowship sponsoring my graduate school was three years long. "Worst case scenario," Bill said, "we'll see each other again in three years' time." His reassurance helped me calm down, though the uncertainty lingered. We would just have to see how things unfolded.

You might have many questions already. How did I get to NASA in the first place? What was I doing in Russia? How does one work on space helicopters for a living and what does that even mean? Why did I choose to get a PhD? When I was just twelve years old, I never would have believed it if you told me I would do even a single one of those things.

Steve Jobs also famously said, "You can only connect the dots looking backward. So you have to trust that the dots will somehow connect in your future." Following his words, let's go back to the beginning and trace how each dot connected on this adventure as I share the lessons I learned along the way.

This is a story of childlike belief, the audacity to choose one's future, and the realization that resilience is our greatest asset. I'm very grateful you found my book and are giving me some of your time. I delayed bringing it to the world for over seven years with the excuse that I was too busy. But in reality, I simply wasn't ready to tell the story since I had not yet fully internalized its meaning.

There's no sugar coating the setbacks, disappointments, and long years of struggle. My victories are celebrated as well, but in writing this book I've come to realize that my greatest growth was born from times of painful failure.

I want nothing more than for this book to have a positive influence on the way you approach your own life. At the very least, I believe you will find it an entertaining memoir of what's possible when you *'Dare to Dream'*. And maybe for a small percentage of you, just maybe, the words in these pages can be the inspiration needed to forever alter the trajectory of your life in the most amazing way possible. I wish that for you and I am rooting for you. Good luck.

Ad astra per aspera,

Jason K. Cornelius

Dr. Jason K. Cornelius
July 2nd, 2024
San Francisco, CA

1. AN ASTRONAUT'S GOLD VISOR

"The future belongs to those who believe in the beauty of their dreams."
— Eleanor Roosevelt

I was interested in all things engineering from the time I was little. Before I even knew what an engineer was, I'd spend countless hours lounging on the living room couch just inches away from the TV, watching shows like Mythbusters, How It's Made, and the History Channel. Looking back on it, I'm sure my choice of entertainment was not always as thoroughly enjoyed by the rest of my family. The only one who might have liked them as much as I did was Xavier, my family's Belgian Tervuren. He was getting to be pretty old and enjoyed lounging on the couch with me getting the occasional belly rub. Okay- maybe he wasn't there for Mythbusters.

Xavier and I shared the house with a few other family members that were certainly not as interested in the History Channel. My sister, Chelsea, was a star athlete in our high school and would much prefer watching her favorite players on the Miami Heat. Our older brother Ryan is 5 years older than me, but seemed more into reading than anything else. He had dozens, if not hundreds of books all over the house. They appeared to be mostly fiction, but who knows, I was not much of a reader at that point in my life. The three of us (along with Xavier) lived with our parents in a small town called Mountain Top.

As you might've guessed, Mountain Top really does sit atop a mountain. This would become a repeated joke made by just about every single non-Mountain-Topian to learn the name of my hometown. The population was about 8,000 people as I remember it. It was the type of small-town where you see five people you know on a trip to the grocery store. We only had two of them after all, Mr. Z's and Carone's markets. It never really occurred to me at the time that we had the only Mr. Z's and Carone's market in the world since they were named after someone in the storied past of our small North-Eastern Pennsylvania town.

Mountain Top was originally an industrial town involved in the moving of coal from the Wilkes-Barre Valley and Ashley Plains up to the Susquehanna River where it would be sent on barges all over the country. One of the last remaining coal breakers in the United States was located just at the bottom of the mountain in Ashley, Pennsylvania. It had long been decommissioned by the time I was growing up, and most of its windows were shattered from years of kids being kids. Even though they stopped using it decades earlier, it was still a historic relic of what created the little place I called home.

My grandfather was pretty into history and an avid reader. If my brother Ryan had dozens of books, my grandfather had hundreds at a minimum. Once I asked him, "Have you actually read all these books?" He chuckled, "No, certainly not. Probably not even half." I'd have to credit my grandfather with giving me a lot of my curiosity for the mechanical and technical side of things. He always seemed to be coming by the house to help us fix one thing or another and he certainly knew how to do it. He had books on 'general construction around the home' and 'how to fix it' where it could be anything. Nowadays I find those books to be quite humorous. They were made in a time before widespread use of the internet put all the 'how-to' knowledge you could ever imagine right at your fingertips, especially now with the advent of technology such as ChatGPT.

One of my mother's favorite stories involving my grandfather is from when

I was just a toddler. My curiosity got me into quite a good bit of trouble growing up. In this particular instance I thought it'd be funny to combine my curiosity with a prank on my mom. I lifted the floor vent for the heat duct and hid inside. I sent her into a panic as she searched the entire house for me. Let's just say she had good reason to believe I could find my way into trouble even at that age. She called my grandmother who lived all the way across town to come over and help look for me. Just as she was about to call the police, she heard a faint giggle coming from beneath the grate.

Sure enough, my grandfather came over that evening to screw all the grates in the house securely to the floor so my mischievous toddler hands couldn't pry them up again. I sat next to him in my diaper and watched him work, curious about the tools and screws he was using.

When I wasn't watching one of my many educational TV shows, I'd often be building and playing with Legos or tearing apart broken electronics in the hope of fixing them. The capacitors, relays, and resistors inside were all things I learned about on TV. Unfortunately, I was never too great at the 'putting them back together' aspect. Still, I had an unquenchable curiosity and wild imagination.

I did well in school but sometime early on I was rejected from my elementary school's gifted program, which was basically a fast track for students showing the most promise. My brother Ryan was a shining pupil at our school and was always in that group of smart students. I don't think I knew it at the time, but I perceived the rejection as 'you are not smart enough to be here.' I didn't fully know what to make of it. I looked up to my brother quite a lot and wanted to be just like him, and at the age of six or seven, life put us on diverging paths.

I spent a lot of time with my grandmother back then. She watched us often when both my mom and dad were working. We became extremely close during the years when Ryan and Chelsea were both in school, and it was just me and her at home. We'd occasionally be late picking up the other two after school as we lost track of time playing checkers, which she recalled I often beat her at from that young age. She knew what that initial rejection meant to me. "Don't you worry, they'll all see someday," she'd often say. What are they going to see? I pondered that question as she continued to say the phrase well into my teenage years. It would take nearly 15 years from her first declaration until I saw it for myself.

Although I was still quite young, the rest of my years in elementary school saw me drifting on a slow downward spiral. I was getting into more and more trouble at school, and probably just as much trouble at home. My friends and I would often play with fireworks—very serious fireworks, if we're being honest, by the time we were done mixing and matching them. We strapped roman candles to my old go-kart and took turns driving around the yard chasing the rest of the group.

This was before the major video games came out such as HALO and Call of Duty, so we had to find creative ways to entertain ourselves. Luckily we were pretty into airsoft, which was the real-world version of those video games before they became commonplace in everyones' living room. We'd run around the yard and woods setting scenarios and just having an all-around blast with it. Only once in a blue moon would someone get injured badly enough that we'd need to call a truce and find an adult.

Playing deep in the woods was probably a bit foolish looking back on it now. The forests surrounding Mountain Top are home to black bears, coyotes, rattlesnakes, and mountain lions. Ticks were the hardest to spot but probably most likely to do us damage whether it be psychological or physical. If you don't know about ticks, consider yourself lucky. They're a small insect that latches onto your skin and then sucks your blood. As they suck your blood, they can swell to the size of a grape! They're extremely hard to remove, especially from a child or dog that's freaking out thanks to the blood-sucking killer. To make matters worse, if you don't remove it carefully, you can pull off just half of it and leave the hypostome (a barbed needle-like structure used to anchor the tick into their host) still embedded. Okay- enough of the gore.

Around this time, I was going to the principal's office at a rate of about once every few months. Fairview Elementary School was set up like a pod structure; each of the six grades had its own pod extending out from a central building that housed the cafeteria, gym, and the principal's office. This made it even more embarrassing to go there because the entire school could see you, not just your own classmates. Some of those visits were probably not warranted, while others certainly were. I once turned a pop-a-point pencil into a blow gun in music class. In my opinion, that was one of the unwarranted ones. If you asked me today to predict the trajectory of a kid in my shoes, I would certainly not say he was on his way to the stars, or even a good university for that matter.

Luckily one day I was in the car with my mom driving. This story is now about 17 years old in my memory, and yet I recall it vividly. My mom was telling me a fun fact she recently heard about an astronaut's helmet. As it turns out, the helmet's visor has a thin covering of gold over it to protect the spacewalker's eyes from harmful cosmic radiation. The gold-plated visor reflects this harmful radiation and also reduces glare so they can see better during spacewalks.

For some reason, twelve-year-old me was so intrigued by this seemingly random fact that I went home and looked it up on our family computer. This was back when having a single desktop computer in my rural Pennsylvania home was still a pretty big deal. The computer had a dial-up connection which meant it made a bunch of 'beeps' and 'boops' when you first turned it on before you could connect to the internet to actually do anything. That 'start-up' time that seemed to take an eternity was maybe only five to ten minutes, which I guess might as well be an eternity by today's standards.

I finally opened a web browser—no google chrome or anything fancy like that. Oh no, we were rocking some good ole fashioned Internet Explorer 7. I searched the astronaut's visor to learn more about it, but back then searching on the internet was a bit of a haphazard task. If you didn't type out exactly the correct prompt, you would get totally unrelated results. I didn't do too badly the first few tries and quickly stumbled upon relevant pages. **What I hadn't expected, however, is that one of those web pages would have a simple word that would alter the course of my life forever.** I was on a Wikipedia page about the astronaut suit when I saw an interesting link to another page titled "Aerospace Engineering." Curiosity got the best of me and I clicked it. What popped up was probably the coolest web-page in existence in 2006. It had images of rockets, airplanes, helicopters, and even NASA!

It was at that exact moment that twelve-year-old me decided I would grow up to become an Aerospace Engineer and someday work at NASA. My little pea-brain couldn't quite comprehend it at the time, but my entire life was about to take on a whole new meaning.

I had fallen a bit off the wagon in the last years of elementary school, at least by my own standards. I didn't do too poorly on my report card, but it certainly was not an A-student performance. I was a pretty funny kid, however, and leveraged my ability to quickly craft jokes and create humor to my advantage. When it came time to graduate from elementary school, the class awarded superlatives at one of the final events of the school year. Given my recent drive to become an aerospace engineer, the coveted superlative may have been 'most likely to succeed.'

My less than stellar grades, antics, and playful demeanor, however, earned me the 'class clown' superlative. I did not find it funny; instead I vividly remember the anger I felt. I wasn't sure whether I should be mad at my classmates for voting for it, or at the teachers for allowing a degrading superlative to be in the mix. Even at this young age, I recognized the path I was on didn't lead in the direction I wanted to go.

My elementary school graded on a quarterly basis, such that we'd have four grades throughout the school year and the final overall year's grade was an average of your four quarters. That final quarter at Fairview Elementary was the first in a number of years that I earned perfect straight A's. I can't say I tried exceptionally hard to get it, but I do very much remember consciously thinking, "Okay- this is the new standard from here on out." The following year, I was off to 7th grade in the big kids' school, which is where this journey truly begins.

As an aside, the kid that got the 'most likely to succeed' award, Ravi, was one of my best friends from the time we were in kindergarten. His family moved to my hometown from India midway through the school year. I remember Ravi's first day quite vividly because I was playing with a toy firetruck when he entered the classroom. I asked him a simple light-hearted five year old type of question, "Do you want to play with the firetruck too?" "Ok," came his short and timid response. At that very moment we became friends for life- boys are really that simple. Ravi's now an anesthesiologist, so I guess the award was fitting.

What did all this mean for me though? I set the goal to work for NASA—which was undoubtedly the dream for millions of kids around the world looking to the stars each night. Oftentimes when we first get an exciting or forward thinking idea, we can be extremely energized by it. We're somewhat blind to the all possible ways it could go wrong or common beliefs that usually stop people from even trying. Initially, I held a childlike belief that it would work out for me. I would soon discover, however, that if you're going to pursue a childlike dream, you should be prepared to face some serious pushback. Only time would tell if I could stand that pressure and create the future I envisioned for myself.

CHALLENGE 1

Defining Your Goal

Get out a sheet of paper (or use the notes section in the back of this book), and write down the goals, aspirations, or dreams you've had throughout life that you decided not to pursue. Maybe they seemed too big, or maybe you feared what others would think of you pursuing them. There's no age limit to success; Colonel Sanders first hit it big with Kentucky Fried Chicken at the age of 62. So, are there any goals or dreams that still excite you? We're looking for ones that have a pulling power on your soul—the ones that speak to you in a way that's hard to explain. If so, put a big circle around it and we'll come back to this a bit later.

2. BUILDING MOMENTUM

"The journey of a thousand miles begins with one step."

— Lao Tzu

Starting middle school was a big change for any kid in Mountain Top. It brought about new friends, experiences, and difficulties associated with teenage life. Over the next few years, I would explore different social circles while I navigated sports, academics, and my own family life. Still, I was energized by the thoughts of aerospace engineering and NASA, and excited to see where it would lead. I had very little idea how I would get there, but that didn't seem like much of an obstacle at the time. All it requires to move towards a goal is a decision, and a small initial step towards it.

My town's two elementary schools combined in the much bigger primary school located in the center of town. Fairview and Rice Elementary Schools had an odd rivalry, even though we hardly ever interacted. I knew a few of the kids from soccer and karate, but for the most part this was the first time we would meet many of the kids from the other school. It was odd going from a place where you were one of the bigger kids in the building to again being one of the tiniest. Everything was bigger: the kids, the lockers, the desks—even the teachers seemed larger.

Luckily for me, the middle and high school buildings were connected, which meant my older siblings were just a short walk away. My brother was in the 98th percentile for male height and my sister's reputation on the basketball court scared people as well. So from that perspective, I felt like I had a pretty good setup. This was the first time we were all in the same building since we were in elementary school together five years earlier. My brother was a senior, though, so we'd only have one more year with all three of us together again. This was a bit of a sad realization; despite the large age gap, we were pretty close for most of our childhood. We'd have to make the best of it.

The best part of starting middle school was organized sports. We now had the ability to join the track, soccer, football, baseball, or tennis teams. I had played soccer since I was little, but I wasn't great and wasn't much of an athlete. My sister got those genetics from my dad who played basketball all his life and was in the 99th percentile for men's height. I guess I got my mom's genes on that one. I had started taking karate in 5th grade and enjoyed all the discipline it was adding to my life. That was one of the many things Ryan did first that I quickly followed. The discipline it instilled in me definitely contributed to me getting more serious in school. Still, I figured it would be fun to do one of the team sports as well.

I decided to go with athletics, which was called track and field in my Northeastern PA dialect. This choice was partially because my body mass index (BMI) suggested I was 6 inches too short for my weight. I was a pudgy kid and wanted to change. I would learn many times over the years that periods of drastic change can occur when you tie several initiatives together to move you in a positive direction.

I'll never forget my first year of track. Our junior varsity team had two coaches: Evan was a bit of a jock and maybe 10 years older than me. Fred, a Marine, was even a few years older than Evan. The day we chose our events, I told them, "I'm going to become a pole vaulter." It seemed the most fun and was more exciting than other events. "Are you being serious?" Evan exclaimed as he poorly hid his laughter. I suppose it was because I was short, chubby, and slow. Much later in life, I'd come to realize the world is full of people like Evan. Luckily, though, the world also has a couple Freds. He was somehow able to see past all the obstacles in my way and simply said, "If you want to do it, then do it." **Sometimes in life we meet unique individuals who can see things for us even when we can't quite see it for ourselves.** Fred was one of those people.

Since pole vaulting was more of a side event early on, especially with practice being governed by Pennsylvania's emergence from Winter, I spent the majority of my time running distance. This turned out to be one of my best decisions of middle-school as we worked our way up to a 45-60 minute daily jog. If you've ever wondered how to lose weight quickly, that will do the trick. I lost about 20% of my body weight in just a few short months. I'd been pole vaulting a bit throughout the season as well, and although I was deplorable, I was getting faster, stronger, and lighter. **I was making progress.**

Middle school was also around the time that I started working odd jobs around the neighborhood to make some money. My family was most definitely middle-class, so as kids we didn't want for much. Still, it was easy for me to see the financial strain on my parents of supporting three teenagers. I didn't really like asking for money, and maybe even more so I didn't like that what I could or couldn't have was decided by someone else. So I put my entrepreneurial spirit to work and decided it was time to make some money.

Pennsylvania requires you to be 16 to work legally, but luckily Mountain Top is not the land of following all the rules. I was old enough to work under the table and that's exactly what I did. Chelsea's basketball league always needed people to run the score-board and I was usually dragged along to her games anyway; so I figured I might as well make some money in the process. I often had parents enraged with me as I became easily distracted talking with friends and added points to the wrong team. Some of them took their kids' sports a bit too seriously.

At 16, I also started working as a dishwasher at one of our local pizzerias.

Mountain Top had a lot of two things: banks and Italian restaurants. The owners of this one were 1st generation immigrants from Naples, and let me tell you they made some amazing food. My mom was a bit hesitant for me to take a real job, thinking it would conflict with school and that it was unfair since Ryan hadn't worked in high school. I convinced her that I just wanted some extra spending money, and school really wasn't too hard for me. I'd held straight A's since that last elementary school report card.

I eventually decided to use a large chunk of my savings to buy a dirt bike for use just around the yard- that's at least how I sold the idea to my mom. Chris, one of my best friends since childhood, and I had other plans. We'd take the dirt bike and go-kart along the train tracks in front of my house until it intersected with the power lines, which were exhilarating to ride on and stretched for miles. You could actually ride them to the next town over, except that the go-kart wouldn't make it up the some of the steeper cliff faces.

You'd get in major trouble though if the Game Wardens caught you riding around out there. They carried Glocks, so they were more like the police than wildlife conservationists. Whenever we saw another car, ATV, or any other semblance of life out there, we'd pull an immediate 180 and move as fast as we could all the way back to my house. We'd usually lose them cutting in and out of the train tracks.

When we weren't evading the Game Wardens, Chris and I could be found around the yard blowing things up. We both had a keen interest in fireworks and I grew up on the outskirts of town, literally in the middle of a forest. Another one of my favorite hobbies was model rocketry, which seemed to go hand-in-hand with the fireworks. My mom or dad would drive me down the street to a large open field to launch them. It was thrilling watching them punch off the pad and I wondered if I'd make the real ones some day. With each launch I could feel my dream picking up some momentum.

As it turned out, I'd soon start working for a professional pyrotechnics company that put on fireworks displays all across the tri-state area. It was a mix of wanting to make more money, and that it was the coolest job I could think of. It was a hard and dangerous job- but the pay was good and it was a blast, literally. We hand lit a majority of the shells with road flares and a few employees had a shell explode in the tube next to them, sending them flying to the ground. I never told my mom about those incidents, and luckily it never happened to me.

Ninth grade came with a few more perks as we transitioned from middle school to high school. One such perk that no doubt shaped my future was an elective class called Integrated Technology. The class was meant to prepare you for a technology degree or maybe even engineering if you were determined enough. With the way we behaved, it felt more like a wood shop class for the nerdy kids.

The classroom had a large white rectangular table that we all sat around waiting for the teacher. I was already friends with most of the kids in the class. It was a bit more career focused and we were getting to the age where you start thinking about what you might want to do for the rest of your life.

In the first week, our teacher Mr. Simmons asked the group, "What do you want to do when you grow up?" When my turn came I naturally told everyone, "I'm going to become an aerospace engineer and work for NASA." What I hadn't counted on was the amount of ridiculing and jostling I'd receive from classmates who simply couldn't see how someone from our little hometown could grow up to someday work for NASA. "Do you know anyone that works at NASA?" they asked. "Do you even know where NASA is? Have you ever met someone that works for NASA?" If becoming an aerospace engineer sounded far-fetched, then working for NASA seemed less likely than winning the lottery. Life has many people like my track coach Evan. It was good training for the future; kids can be particularly direct and blatantly mean. With all my crazy ideas to come, it would be necessary to develop tough skin.

We definitely had the most fun in that class as we learned some of the fundamentals of circuitry and various other mechanical concepts. The really fun days came when we'd use the electronics station to light the graphite core of a pencil on fire.

We liked to keep the substitute teachers on their toes, and wouldn't dare do it with Mr. Simmons. I'd say we were actually quite fortunate to have him as a teacher. He had exposure to some engineering careers and although once in a while he'd join in on the jostling, I vividly remember him standing up for me when they teased me for my dream to work at NASA. "You guys keep laughing, he's going to be your boss some day." Mr. Simmons also randomly shouted "bumble bee tuna" and "slim-slow," however, so I wasn't sure whether or not I should believe him.

Freshman year was also the first time Chris and I decided to go out for football. We did most things together, so I convinced him to go on that crazy adventure with me as well. It's pretty tough starting football at an older age since everyone else has been playing since four or five years old. Even the kids that are smaller than you have better technique, know how to block, tackle, and generally whip your butt up and down the field. That season of football was one of the most challenging times of my adolescent life. Chris was on the larger side and could take care of himself, so he was mostly left alone. I was not particularly tall on the other hand, and was now skinny thanks to track. Several kids on the team seemed to have fun putting me to shame in practice.

Being somewhat quick and skinny meant I'd be a wide receiver and corner. That was generally awful since I wasn't great at catching the ball and would go flying whenever I got hit at high speed. One practice, I was speared in the chest by our team captain- a very dangerous and illegal move in football. I remember jumping back up off the ground and having the strangest sensation- I couldn't breathe at all. He knocked the wind out of me so badly that seconds later, I collapsed on the field. It turned out his girlfriend broke up with him so he was looking to take out some anger. Another time we were practicing in the snow, and one of the biggest guys on the team was blocking for the running back behind him. I tried to go up against him, got launched into the air, slammed onto the cold hard field, and skidded at least 20 feet on its icy surface before coming to a stop.

Football wasn't for me- that much I was certain about. I knew I had big goals, though, and being a quitter was not part of the plan. Although I hated that season of football 80% of the time, I finished it out because of my own principles. My dad would throw the ball around with me every so often in the yard so I could work on catching. Xavier played a good corner chasing me around as I tried to snag it out of the air. I wouldn't say I became good at it, but I was at least able to catch a pass once in a while instead of swatting each one to the ground.

Those few months taught me some valuable lessons about life: 1) don't commit to something unless you're sure you want to do it, and 2) if you commit to something you better just make up your mind that you want to do it. This set some good precedents for my young-adult life that I would most definitely soon be in need of.

Around this time, I also started participating in the Pennsylvania Junior Academy of Science. PJAS is a science fair where students from 7th-12th grade compete by giving a presentation to a panel of judges on a STEM topic of their choosing. It was like the nerd olympics. One of my oldest friends, Megan, was a grade below me and convinced me to get into the competition. She was a family friend and we knew each other since we were about three.

My first year in the competition I chose electro-magnetism. The regional competition took place first with students from neighboring high schools. Now if you scored well enough to get a first place award at this regional competition, you were invited to go to the state competition. So as you can imagine the stakes were high. I gave my presentation using physical slides on an overhead projector. We had to be one of the last groups of students in America to be making and using overhead transparencies for a presentation.

The judging panels consisted of volunteers from various STEM fields. After I presented my slides describing the science behind electromagnets, one of the judges asked me to give an example application of one. In a moment of desperation, I looked at the ceiling and thankfully saw a speaker. I very eloquently (at least it felt that way at the time), explained that the speaker above us operated using the principles of an electromagnet by pulsating a membrane back and forth to make acoustic pressure waves creating the sound that reaches our ear. The explanation was so off the cuff, that I earned not only a first place, but also a perfect score. I earned myself a trip to the state competition, which just so happened to be at The Pennsylvania State University (aka: Penn State).

Megan and I, along with a few other classmates in our studious (some might say nerdy) circle, made the trip to Penn State several times over the years. Although we were at Penn State to compete, it was also a fun time to explore the campus. The state competition was held over the summer meaning that we got to stay in the freshman dorms on a relatively quiet campus. We walked around campus imagining what college would be like someday. Megan and I hung around each other a lot at these competitions though at the time I was too foolish to pick up the hints.

Despite starting as a nerdy, chubby kid, I did okay with the girls. I suppose it helped that I was funny, smart, had gotten into solid shape, and did well on the track team. (I was pole vaulting 11 feet by this point—take that, Evan).

My sixteenth birthday also came with an exciting surprise. My parents got me a discovery flight at our local airport. The Forty Fort airport (officially called the Wilkes-Barre Wyoming Valley airport) is a general aviation airport about thirty minutes from Mountain Top. For a discovery flight, you basically pay a commercial pilot to take you up for an hour of flying. Most people do it to see if they're interested in getting their pilots license.

I don't remember whose idea this birthday present was; though if I had to guess I'd say my dad's since my mom would be (and is) far too afraid of the idea of me flying in a small plane. So one day a few weeks later, my dad and I went to the local airport and met our pilot. He was an old retired military airman—the kind that seemed like he had many stories to tell. As scary as flying in this little plane could seem, it was somehow easy to trust your life to a guy like this.

I was asking a million questions the entire time. I'd learned some of the most basic principles of flight from TV, movies, and YouTube videos. Eventually we got into the plane, which was a 4-seater Cessna 172 Skyhawk. The pilot and I were sitting up front, and my dad squished in the back seat having to duck his head a bit so as to not hit it on the roof.

We were lined up at the end of the three-thousand-foot asphalt runway. The engine noise was loud, but all three of us had headsets on, allowing us to communicate over the radio. "Are you ready?" came the direct-to-the-point question from the pilot. "Yes." was my equally short one word reply. "Put your hand on this black knob, and when I tell you, push it in and keep it there." was the instruction from the pilot. "Okay." I had many follow-up questions about the task at hand and what we were doing, but it didn't seem like the right time for chit-chat.

His instructions were clear enough, and when he said go, I gently put the throttle to full and held it there for dear life. He came over the headset, "Okay, no turning back now." As we accelerated down the runway, my brain was moving a mile a minute. Before I even knew what happened, we were peeling off the runway and moving away from the ground. It was one of the craziest sensations I'd ever experienced. Everyone was quiet for a few short seconds as we took in these strange new sensory feelings. I held the throttle in place so firmly that I noticed my hand beginning to hurt—so be it. We weren't dying on my watch.

The pilot eventually told me I could let go of the throttle, and we enjoyed an amazing ride over the entire Wyoming Valley. We flew South to Mountain Top and circled over the high school. It was amazing how much something changes when you see it from another perspective. He gave me a try at the controls, walking me through how to steer the plane. By the time we touched back down on the ground I had made up my mind—this was definitely the coolest thing I had ever done.

The experience further increased my desire to study aerospace and make a career working on things that fly. I came to another realization that day as well; I would most certainly be getting my pilot's license someday. I knew it was a goal that would have to wait a considerable amount of time since becoming a pilot is an expensive endeavor. Typically it's around 10-20 thousand dollars with everything included, which was certainly not in my immediate future.

I still had an immensely long journey ahead to achieve my goals, but I was taking the first steps towards them. Each week I was learning more about aerospace, becoming more fit and better at pole vault, and having a blast along the way. All these things, however, were about to be unexpectedly placed very far on the backburner.

CHALLENGE 2

Building Momentum

You identified some goals or aspirations that you currently have or previously had for your life. (If you didn't complete Challenge 1, you can go back and do it now). Identify one skill or habit that would start moving you in a positive direction. Even if it's not your one single goal from Challenge 1, what can you start doing today that would move you in the direction you want to go? Make it simple, and just choose one thing. When we focus our energy towards a single aim, mighty forces come to our aid. Start working towards it, and be proud that you're taking steps to aim up in life. Just beginning to act is half the battle.

3. WHEN LIFE KNOCKS YOU DOWN

"Sometimes life is going to knock you flat on your back. Make sure you have enough reason to keep on keepin on."

— Les Brown

Some of life's hardest pills to swallow are those that feel unjust or unfair. Every so often, the universe delivers a blow that tests our morale and spirit. These moments, as terrible as they are, offer a choice—a fork in the road. We can either retreat to the safety of what we know or push forward, fueled by a deeper dedication to our higher selves. One of these defining moments came at the end of my junior year, a chaotic time that shook my world. I had to decide if I'd let it keep me down or find the strength to move forward.

It was near the end of my junior year of high-school. I was succeeding across multiple endeavors including becoming quite successful in track and field, having received my black belt in karate, and generally having a great time with my friends at school as we prepared to go into the adventure that would be senior year. Chelsea had already gone off to college, but was just 45 minutes away and often came home on the weekends. We had started becoming closer as we grew older. As kids, I had much more in common with my brother, but during my sister's last year of high school, we drove to and from school together almost every day.

One day, the classroom I was in received a phone call. My sister was there early to check me out of school. Although a bit out of the ordinary, we did these things sometimes to just go grab food so I didn't think much of it. When I met her out front of the school though, I learned that life was about to take a pretty wicked turn.

My mom had been a labor and delivery nurse since she was about 20. She put herself through an associates degree in nursing at the local community college, studying while holding a job to pay her bills. By the time I hit high school she had switched to night-shift because she felt like she was missing too much of her time with us. This meant she'd leave around dinner, work all night, and then be at home in the morning to help us get ready for school. I honestly had no idea how she did it all—she was supermom—until it became too much.

A bit earlier that morning before my sister checked me out of school, my mom fell asleep behind the wheel just two minutes from our house after her 30 minute commute home from work. The car drifted off the road, rolled through a telephone pole, and landed upside down in the woods. We never found out who called, but a quick response time saved her life. When the first responders arrived on scene, she was hanging upside down in the car unconscious with blood dripping out of her head.

Mountain Top was a small enough town that one of the first responders on scene knew my mom and was talking to her hoping she could hold on for just a bit longer. The fire department used the Jaws of Life to cut the crushed car door off and extract her from what used to be a Honda CR-V. She was taken via ambulance to the nearest major hospital, which was a town over in Wilkes-Barre. Upon her arrival, an entire trauma team went to work trying to save her life.

Chelsea told me there was an accident when she picked me up. We raced home, thinking we'd meet my dad there before heading to the hospital. Despite their marriage issues (it was evident to me by this point that a divorce was inevitable), he was clearly shaken up by the whole thing as well. We sat at the house for a while before heading to the hospital. I think he thought he was doing the best thing by keeping us busy while she was in the emergency room, but it probably would have been better if we were waiting there instead.

On our way to the hospital, he warned us that it might be a bit frightening to see her. When we arrived, my uncle and aunt who had also both been in the medical field comforted us while trying to prepare us for what we were about to see. We entered the room to find her face so swollen it was nearly unrecognizable. She had IV's pumping fluids into her, and several other machines monitoring her. I stood against the wall while Chelsea immediately went to her side and began to cry. She lifted her hand slightly in an attempt to wave me over, not really being able to speak. It took all my courage to walk up to the bedside and hold her hand.

My mom was released from the hospital a few days later and would be out of work for the next several weeks as she rested and recovered. With her being on the path to recovery, life gradually returned to a new normal, and I refocused on my goals at school.

A few weeks after her car crash, we went to the local car dealership and picked a new car out for her. She financed a Honda CR-V, the same car model that had saved her life.

A few days later, we returned to the dealership and she took on another loan so I could get a three year old Honda Civic. My mom had gotten both my brother and sister their first cars, and she was too proud of that fact to let me get the short end of the stick. It was a tough time; the accident was still fresh, and now she was going to be taking on two new car payments. Although we were by no means poor, I started to see more clearly the financial situation we were in.

My brother and sister were both off at college, which my mom took out loans to help them pay for. Then here I was at a car dealership allowing her to finance an almost new car. At one point, I went out to my mom's new CR-V to get our insurance card. I leaned against the wall outside and fought back tears. At this point I really wasn't in a position to contribute financially, and that bothered me to my core. I swore right then and there that I would do everything in my power to turn that around.

By this point, I had started working at McDonald's as a cashier. I had already been working as a dishwasher for a good year or so, but decided switching to McDonalds would provide slightly more pleasant working conditions. With my steady job and reliable hours, I knew I could help, even if just a little, with the car payments. From that point on, I made it a goal to ask for money as rarely as possible, relying instead on my own earnings.

As senior year at Crestwood High School rolled around, that independence grew. My friends and I were now working jobs, had some cash in our pockets, and had found ways to navigate both the school system and the freedom that came with driving.

Senior year also had what we called "the young scholars" program. The top 15 or 20 percent of the class was able to start the mornings by taking college level courses at one of three local colleges. I use the term 'local' sparingly since the closest one was 10 miles from our high school. We would carpool together down the mountain into Wilkes-Barre, which was the next town over. Only the top few percent of students were able to have their pick between the two 4-year colleges, whereas the rest would take classes at the 2-year community college. Despite having straight A's from that decisive day in sixth grade, my class standing was hurt by the fact that I took the Integrated Technology classes. Other students loaded up on courses like AP Spanish and European History that were weighted heavier and boosted their class standing. Still, I made it into the top group by the skin of my teeth and would go to King's College in Wilkes-Barre.

I carpooled with two girls: one of whom lived just down the street from me, and the other we had both known since kindergarten. At Kings I took psychology and public speaking. Psychology was an absolutely fascinating course, and you could tell the professor loved nothing more than to teach us all the seemingly crazy facets of the human mind. A lot of his examples and previous studies involved rats, and his fascination with them seemed a bit odd to me at the time. The speech class was with this amazing older woman who jumped out of airplanes as a paratrooper in one of the previous US wars. Despite psychology being immensely interesting, speech class was where I had the most fun and really shined. I remember she called me "hot dog." I can still hear her voice, "Okay hot dog- you're funny, which is rare, but don't wear it out." This was her constructive feedback after one of my humor infused speeches about the behavior of guys in the gym.

Senior year at Crestwood was also the first time you could take physics. At the time, only about 40-50 students out of our class of 270 took it. A man named Mr. Garraui, who had been teaching physics in my hometown for quite some time, taught the class. Mr. Garroui was born in Tunisia, and was one of the very few foreigners I had ever met. The overwhelming majority of Mountain Top consisted of white anglo saxon protestants, or WASPS, as my grandmother would often tell me. The only real racial or ethnic diversity we had was a few families of Gujaratis (from the Gujarat state of India) that had all seemed to follow each other to our little rural town. The Gujarati students were always top of the class and were good friends and friendly competition. We all took physics with Mr. Garraoui.

Mr. Garraui was an intriguing man. He had many interesting phrases and quotes that I imagine were translations from Arabic proverbs. A lot of them didn't make sense but we found them humorous and he could always keep our attention despite the difficult subject matter. One of his quotes, however, was crystal clear. "Work hard for the next four years, and the rest of your life will be easy."

There were a handful of us that were very serious about our future career plans, and knew that the Physics Advanced Placement (AP) exam would help us in the long run. Passing this test allowed you to skip the introductory courses at university, effectively giving you a head start. The problem, however, was that even the basic physics class was already difficult enough for most students. It was not enough to prepare us for the AP exam. A few of us met and asked Mr. Garraoui if he could help us. After some careful consideration, he explained to the six of us the task we'd be signing up for.

We would have to come into school on Saturday mornings to study with him since the material on the AP exam went so much further than what we covered in our introductory class. We'd spend our study halls going into his classroom to do practice problems. Throughout our training, he taught us how to get a 'good enough score' to pass—there simply wasn't enough time to master the material. This meant that some problems, we wouldn't even attempt to solve and would just skip right over them leaving more time for the ones that we had studied.

We agreed to his terms, and the next several weeks and months would turn out to be a lot of fun as we had our personal tutoring sessions. Mr. Garroui volunteered his time out of the goodness of his own heart; he wasn't getting paid anything extra to be there with us on weekends. He knew the group had a hunger for knowledge and the pursuit of our goal, he was an educator with the background needed to enable us to succeed, and that's all that mattered to him.

When it came time for the AP Physics exam in the spring, our entire group earned the highest marks possible, even though our school didn't offer an AP Physics class. At the time, it felt like we had pulled off the first movie-worthy miracle. Just one more to go.

The spring also brought track season, which proved to be another excellent way for me to develop my mental grit and determination. I had become a force to be reckoned with in the pole vault arena by this point. I cleared 11' 9" the season prior and had my sights set on the school record which was still a good bit out of reach at 13' and some change. Not too bad for a kid that only a few years earlier was too short, slow, and chubby to be a realistic contender in the eyes of some.

My high school activities—track, karate, and more—had turned me into a lean machine. Before this point I was not fast enough to be competitive with the older kids in sprinting. But now that I was the oldest, I figured I might have at least some bit of a shot. I ended up getting into the 100-meter dash and the 4x400-meter relays. I don't think I ever won a heat of the 100-meter dash, but somehow our relay team turned out to be pretty successful. Truth be told, we had ourselves a secret weapon: Marty.

I first met Marty in seventh grade when we both arrived in middle school. His mom taught at the other elementary school, and his house was about as far as one could get from my house within our school district. We were also both on the track team together since seventh grade and took the Integrated Technology classes. So we spent quite a good bit of time together both inside and out of school. No matter where we were, we tried our best to stay out of trouble (or at least evade getting caught).

So Marty and I were also both on the 4x400-meter relay team. This involves each member of the four person team sprinting the baton one lap around the track. It's a long enough race for plenty of opportunity for leads to be made, lost, and won back again. In my opinion, it's the most exciting event, maybe only second to pole vault.

It was our final meet of the season and the score between us and the opposing team was tight. In order for us to win the meet, I'd have to take 1st in pole vault and 1st in the 4x400-meter relay with Marty and the others.

The pole vault event was long and we were up around 11' 9" when it came time for the relay. I had to check out with the official, who would pause the pole vault competition just long enough for me to run an all out sprint around the track before returning to vault.

As the starting gun went off, our first runner bolted out on the first lap around the track and it was clear we were going to have our work cut out for us. As the baton changed hands the first time going into lap 2, we were just a few paces ahead. There's a good bit of strategy in how you order the runners for relay teams, and this time around our opponent put their best runner second.

While they raced around the track, they began to take a commanding lead. It was looking pretty ugly, but then again, we had our secret weapon. Marty, as per usual, sprinted near full-speed the entire way around the track, handed off the baton, and then immediately went to the nearest garbage can to vomit. The important thing today was that he not only caught up to the third leg of the opposing team, but even gained a bit of a lead before handing the baton off to our last runner, me.

Me being the final runner of our 4x400-meter relay team was a fitting end to the several years of hard work and dedication to become something others couldn't quite see for me. In the words of my middle-school coach Fred, "If you want to do it, do it."

The team was counting on me. I took off running and around the 250-meter mark I could hear the heels of the opposing runner gaining on me. The rest of the world seemed to go silent as my brain focused on the last 150-meters. To this day I don't know where it came from, but something within me ignited and I was able to turn on the jets. After already running 300-meters, I sprinted full-speed the final stretch of track to win the race. The scene at the finish was electric.

I took a *very* slow walk back over to the pole vault area in an attempt to try and catch my breath. The other competitor had successfully jumped 12' 3" but then failed at 12' 9", which meant if I could clear that height then we would win the final track meet of our senior year. *No pressure.*

The air was warm and the crowd was quiet. Everyone was around the pole vault area to watch this unfold. To them, it was just a track and field meet. To me, it was the culmination of a five-year journey marked with trials and tribulations. Would I use them as a crutch to lean on, or as fuel to drive myself forward?

I took a few huffs and puffs, and then barreled down the track. I didn't plant the pole well and crashed into the bar—there went my first of three attempts. On attempt two I had a good jump but grazed the bar and knocked it down. There was just one more try left.

I took what felt like several minutes of mental zen time at the far end of the track, staring at the battle before me. It seemed like such an easy thing- just jump over the stupid bar. Pole vault was actually a very technical sport with a lot of physics and mechanics involved. The amount of potential energy stored in the pole at its maximum bend is enough to break your bones if it snaps on you, which happens more often than you would expect.

I took a deep breath. As I started racing down the track the outside world again went silent. It was just me, the pole, the mat that was supposed to catch me, and that stupid bar. I flew over that thing and cleared it by at least five or six inches, it wasn't even close. It took a few seconds after I crashed into the mat to realize that I actually pulled it off. The team was ecstatic – **we had won the meet.**

I would go on to pole vault at the District Track meet where I made it onto the awards podium. I remember seeing my mom in the stands right in front of me. *To her, it was as if I had just won the olympics.*

After graduation, the majority of my 'academic' high school friends headed to several different local Universities. The popular choice given its proximity was Penn State University's (PSU's) Main Campus, not to be confused with the University of Pennsylvania (an Ivy League school near Philadelphia). A lot of my friends chose to stay local, going to King's College, or PSU campuses in Hazleton, Harrisburg, or Wilkes-Barre to save money living at home. For me, I was ready for a new adventure away from the troubles and somewhat unpleasant reality of what had become home.

I would fall out of touch with most of my high school friends, except for Chris and Marty. Some of them, though, including Ravi and Megan, would find their way to Penn State as well.

Although the process was long, my mom would go on to make a near-full recovery. To this day, she still has issues with her back and neck, but it was a good outcome given the seriousness of the situation.

I learned many lessons in high school whether it was from studying Physics with Mr. Garraoui or working to become our school's best pole vaulter. The most important among them, was that whenever I pursued something out of the ordinary, there were always people close-by telling me why it wouldn't work out. Over the years, my goals would become loftier and the naysayers would become more vocal. I suppose at some point I decided that if I'm going to have to listen to them for being out of the ordinary, I might as well go all the way and aim for extraordinary. Nowadays, I patiently listen to their spiel and then try it out anyway. I suggest you do the same. **Don't let other peoples' beliefs stop you from pursuing your dream.**

CHALLENGE 3
Curveballs

Think back to a time when life hit you in the head with a brick. How did you handle it? Was there anything you could have done differently to improve your response or recovery? Bad things will happen to all of us throughout life. But it's how we choose to respond to them that really makes the difference. What specific steps can you take to build resilience for when life throws the next curveball your way?

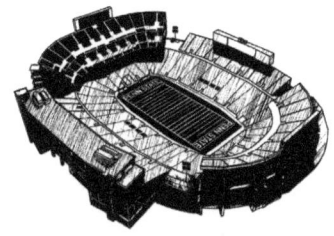

4. PENN STATE – 1 OF 5 WILL GRADUATE

"Nothing in this world can take the place of persistence. Talent will not; nothing is more common than unsuccessful people with talent. Genius will not; unrewarded genius is almost a proverb. Education will not; the world is full of educated derelicts. Persistence and determination alone are omnipotent."

— Former U.S. President Calvin Coolidge

I learned the meaning of this quote during my first semester at Penn State. The competition pool was small enough in my hometown that excelling in things like math and physics was really not that hard. When I arrived at Penn State, however, I quickly realized that I was in a different ballgame. Most of the students in my classes were all top of their high school math and physics classes, and everyone was fighting for a finite number of spots in the program.

One of my friends once said, "It's not that you're incredibly smart; you just work harder than everyone else." At the time, I wasn't sure whether I should be insulted or appreciative of the comment. Looking back on it, though, I see the truth in the sentiment. I've had the good fortune to cross paths with many people much smarter than me over the years, whether it be due to their past experiences, opportunities, or sheer brainpower. Still, what consistently gave me the relative advantage was that I was willing to work harder than the person next to me. No matter what it is that someone chooses to do, I sincerely believe they will achieve it with consistent and dedicated effort.

Having toured countless schools with my brother and sister, I had a solid sense of college life. But after attending a Penn State football game, I knew this was where I wanted to be. Beaver Stadium at PSU, which holds about 110,000 people, creates an absolutely electric experience. On a home football gameday, Penn State becomes the third largest city in Pennsylvania behind only Philadelphia and Pittsburgh. It's safe to say that the atmosphere convinced me PSU was the place to be.

Penn State also had a great aerospace engineering program and I received some scholarship money from my involvement in the PJAS competitions. From my time there for the state competitions, I knew I liked the campus and it was only two hours away from home. Far enough to truly be away, but close enough to come back anytime.

So I only applied to Penn State and figured my odds were reasonably high. PSU also has something called the Schreyer Honors College (SHC), which is only for the top few percent of students in each class. Out of a new freshman class of 10,000 students, maybe 300 would enter as Schreyer Scholars. My math score on the SAT (the US college entrance exam) was in the 99th percentile nationwide, but my reading and writing were only around the 50th percentile. I guess I should have followed in my brother's footsteps on the whole reading thing.

In the end, I was admitted to Penn State's main campus in State College, PA, but I was rejected from SHC. My rejection from SHC stung a good bit, but I still decided to join Penn State in fall of 2013 with an intended major of aerospace engineering.

My real journey at Penn State started with New Student Orientation, colloquially referred to on campus as NSO. Penn State's engineering program has a unique setup. You declare the major you eventually want to get into, in my case aerospace engineering, but you are technically in a pre-major status for the first two years of school. You get put into the actual aerospace program then starting junior year if you make the cut.

At NSO, we had one of the more senior professors from the Department of Aerospace Engineering give us our 'welcome speech.' There were probably about 30 students in the room. He said, "Look at the student behind you, the one in front of you, the one to your left, and the one to your right. Of the five of you, only one will cross the stage at graduation as a Penn State aerospace engineer." The statistic, whether factual or fictitious, was shocking enough to bring each and every one of us firmly back into reality. Each of us would come to terms in our own way with the validity of that statement in due time.

The first semester of Penn State Engineering was brutal. I had Calculus II, Physics I, Chemistry I, Macroeconomics, and a first year seminar. Luckily, my high school training with Mr. Garraui made this first physics class a breeze, but the rest of the schedule was an absolute gauntlet. The first two years at Penn State were meant to weed students out. Essentially eliminating those that wouldn't be able to keep up the pace in the tough engineering majors.

I hadn't realized the increase in difficulty from high school, where I could easily stay at the top, to Penn State, where I'd have to struggle to stay afloat. I was quite naive in the first few weeks: I went to classes, then I came back to the dorms, hung out with friends, and went to parties. I was certainly studying, but studying along the lines of what I was used to in high school (i.e., not that much). My first Calculus exam brought me crashing back down to Earth. I hadn't done too terribly by Penn State engineering standards, but for someone that was used to acing every single exam, a 78 on an exam worth 25% of your final grade came as a bit of a shock.

I met another student early on named Sal. He lived on the same floor as me in the freshman dorms and was an aerospace engineering pre-major as well. Honestly, that's where our similarities ended. Sal was well read and seemed to know a little about almost everything from politics, to finance, to whatever other rabbit holes he explored on Reddit. Sal's global perspective, likely in large part thanks to his parents having immigrated from India, began opening my eyes to a world beyond rural Pennsylvania.

Despite my avid interest in the history channel growing up, I often found myself outgunned against my peers when it came to critical thinking on a wide range of current events and other important topics. Maybe it was really due to where I grew up, or maybe I just didn't care to learn about it back then. I really don't know.

At any rate, Sal and I would have several classes together each semester for the next five years, so we naturally became close in a short matter of time. One of the most motivating things that's ever been said to me in my entire life came directly from Sal. We had just left the dorm one autumn day and were on our way to class. "I think I'm going to apply to the National Science Foundation's Graduate Research Fellowship Program one day." The NSF fellowship is an all expense paid graduate education in a STEM major of your choosing, and it is extremely hard to get.

Sal literally laughed out loud, "Only the best students in the entire university get those." I'm sure he didn't mean much by it, but the words ripped through me like a 50 caliber machine gun. The implication, at least in my mind, was that a small-town kid from Pennsylvania didn't stand a chance. To be fair, his thoughts weren't completely unfounded. To be selected for an NSF award, a student needs to demonstrate both intellectual merit and broader impact on their local community and society. They also exhibit traits such as leadership, drive, resilience, and passion. I had passion, but was so far lacking in almost every other department. Sal was right—it was a half-baked wishy-washy pipe-dream.

It would not be the first time in my life, nor the last, where I thought to myself, "I'll show you." As it turned out, Sal was way ahead of me and would continue to kick my butt for quite a while. We developed a nice and mostly friendly rivalry, which no doubt helped to push both of us to higher heights and achievement. In his first semester, he was already doing independent research in the aerospace department's wind energy program. I was so dull I didn't even realize this was an option.

Hearing about Sal's research inspired me to start looking into research opportunities myself. I went on the aerospace department's website and looked at various professors, skimming their biographies and research interests to try and identify one to reach out to. Most of their biographies were so convoluted with technical jargon, to me at least, that they might as well have been in another language.

I eventually settled on a handful to email and wrote something to the effect of, 'Do you have any undergraduate research positions?' Blunt and to the point—I was not very sophisticated in those early days. Most of them didn't bother to answer me, and looking back on it now, I really can't blame them. I was one freshman out of over 10,000 joining Penn State that fall with nothing yet to show for it.

One professor, Dr. Ed Smith, emailed back. "Hi Jason. Why don't you stop by my office to discuss this further." Later that week I met the director of Penn State's Vertical Lift Research Center of Excellence (VLRCOE), the person and the institution that would forever alter my future. We had a really nice discussion on many topics ranging from aerospace at Penn State to helicopters and their role in society. Dr. Smith recommended I check out the local student chapter of the American Helicopter Society (now called the Vertical Flight Society). I still pressed him for undergraduate research opportunities, knowing that it was immensely hard to secure an industry internship after freshman year.

Dr. Smith posed a sort of challenge to me, "If you get a 4.0 this first semester, then we can see about getting you a research position in the VLRCOE this summer." A 4.0 sounded pretty optimistic, especially given the poor score I earned on my first calculus exam. To this day I don't know if Dr. Smith says that to students all the time, or maybe he saw something in me that I didn't see in myself at the time. I'll be fine if I never learn the answer to that one. But his challenge sparked something in me—he set a clear target, and now, I was ready to hit it. It was time to hunker down. The cold Penn State Winter was quickly approaching and I was on a mission; two missions to be exact.

In addition to shooting for a 4.0, there was also another grand target I was aiming at in that first semester at Penn State. It was called 'SHC Gateway.' Things at PSU, especially during the snowy wintertime, often took on a mystical air about them. The SHC Gateway was one example of that. It was a back-door admission to the Schreyer Honors College for students that either transferred to Penn State or that didn't get in directly out of high school. To get in, I would have to demonstrate the SHC values, which include academic excellence with integrity, civic engagement, and a global perspective. I would have to hone all these characteristics to have a competitive application, but I decided it would be easiest to just start with one.

I began studying harder and longer than most of my friends at PSU. Every single day after classes I'd take two or three textbooks to what we called 'The Stacks' in the Pattee-Paterno library. The Stacks, a quiet, archive-like section of the library, contained tens of thousands of books, row after row. Much of the library was extremely nice, with modern renovated sections including couches to rest, computer rooms, smart boards, and even a Starbucks. The Stacks, however, were definitely more on the practical side. At the end of the stacks were a row of old wooden desks set up against the windows overlooking Curtain Avenue, which is the top end of campus. I'd sit there studying late into the night every single weekday, going page by page through my calculus, physics, chemistry, and economics books. It was one of the most studious times of my life.

The Stacks were definitely not glamorous, but they were quiet and a very good environment to work in. If you made any noise at all, you'd have 20 pairs of eyes peeking out past their desks' glaring at you. After a long day of classes followed by several more hours of studying, I'd finally pack up and head back to the dorms. But each time, there was one more thing I had to do before calling it a day.

Despite the freezing cold State College winter, I wouldn't walk the quickest path back to the cozy warmth of my dorm room. Instead, I'd go out of my way so that I could walk past the front entrance to the Honors College. I really didn't want to study on many of those late nights. Every time I walked past the entrance to SHC, however, it reminded me that each hour spent in the library was one step closer to achieving my goals. The words of Lao Tzu echoed in my mind.

By the end of the semester, I had secured an A in every class, except Chemistry. This was a notoriously rigorous weed-out class, and my high school hadn't prepared me well for it. We learned the periodic table, how elements come together to form molecules, and much more. When I calculated my grade, I fell just a few tenths of a point shy of an A. It felt like I got punched in the gut as I would just miss the 4.0 that I had I fought so hard for.

Then I learned about something called a curve, which would come to my rescue more than once during my time at Penn State. My Chemistry final grade was bumped up from an A- to an A.

I did it.

I sent one of the proudest emails I can recall to Dr. Smith after the final grades were posted to let him know I received my 4.0. I like to think he was probably shocked and now had to figure out what he would do with some crazy kid he made a deal with several months prior. It was the only 4.0 I ever got at Penn State, and I fought for every single bit of it.

Still, I can't write this story and pretend like all I did was sit in that library each and every day. Although I sure was in there a lot, my group of friends also knew how to have a good time. We adventured all over downtown State College on the weekends and certainly enjoyed the Penn State football games and tailgates.

Although I still had another entire semester to my freshman year, my summer slot in the VLRCOE had been secured. I went home for a few weeks over winter break to equally as cold Mountain Top, PA where my mom and brother were now living in my childhood house. My parents officially separated shortly after I left for Penn State, as if waiting for me to graduate and move out. That meant my first Christmas break from Penn State was a fiasco of trying to satisfy divorcing parents. As my siblings and I would come to learn, it's an idealistic goal that's almost impossible to achieve in practice. My mind was back at Penn State, and soon I would be too.

The spring semester would be another hard one with more calculus, physics, Engineering Design, and a first year seminar. First year seminars at Penn State are a type of course meant to expose you to your major early, or sometimes just expose you to something you find particularly interesting.

My situation was neither. I had picked a first year seminar about engineering in China because I scheduled so late that nothing else was available. I'll be honest and say that at this point in my life, despite Sal's best efforts, I didn't think too much about what was happening in the rest of the world. Professor Xinli Wu taught the course, and my global perspective was about to get a big overhaul.

The courses this semester were even more challenging than the first one. Calculus III and Physics II were completely new material I never saw in high school. On top of that, my friends and I were now more connected around campus and more readily found parties to go to. My good study habits from the first semester would allow me to handle the tough course material, but we all still had to balance our studies with our fun.

A few other pre-engineering friends lived in the freshman dorm with me and Sal: Paul, Pat, Maysoor, and others would become great friends that continued to pop up throughout my journey. We all studied pretty diligently throughout the week but then would meet up in the dorms on Friday night to group up and head downtown. We'd wake up early Saturday and head to the library, then repeat it all again Saturday night and into Sunday.

Things became more challenging when my relationship with a girl I'd started seeing became more serious. She hung around my friend group and was in a sorority, which I thought was kinda cool. Her dorm was adjacent to mine, which proved to be as distracting as you could imagine. We had a lot of fun though and were there for each other throughout the ups and downs of life as 1st year college students.

Compared to the courses that ate pre-engineering students for breakfast, my first year seminar on engineering in China was a very enjoyable experience. Professor Wu showed us videos about various engineering marvels in China as we discussed what life was like over there. The course was relaxed, which was a very nice change of pace from our regularly scheduled programming of equations and calculations.

Dr. Wu also led a one month summer program called, "Impact of Culture on Engineering in China." The program was an experiential travel trip that traversed about 15 major Chinese cities in 30 days. Dr. Wu would have program alumni come to each of his classes to talk about their trip, share their thoughts on China, and generally recommend students to sign up for it. I thought the trip sounded amazing, and Professor Wu really wanted me to join. The only problem was money—and where I could find it. Luckily my high performance in first semester afforded me the opportunity to secure a scholarship or two for the program. Still, it was several thousand dollars and neither me nor my family had that kind of money sitting around to go gallivanting abroad.

I eventually very hesitantly brought up the idea of the trip to my mom. Every part of me wanted to go, but I knew the reality of my financial situation. Being the provider she is, she said she would find a way to do it. My mom drove to Penn State to meet Dr. Wu since it would be the first time 'her baby' left the United States. Xinli was one of the most genuine and caring people I'd ever had the opportunity to meet. My mom immediately felt at ease about the trip, and we decided to sign me up for it.

In the end, I would have to take out some additional student loans for the trip, she picked up extra shifts at the hospital, and family and friends would chip in to send me on my way.

Throughout the rest of the spring, word of the trip spread among my friend group, which was mostly engineering students after all. Both my girlfriend and my friend Paul from the dorm floor would sign up for the trip and join me in China.

The rest of the semester was filled with the typical freshman year adventures, shenanigans, and exams. We worked hard and played hard. Some of the kids in our group would learn that they played too hard and realize this first year at Penn State would be their last. For me, the semester came to a successful conclusion, albeit without another 4.0. I had gotten into a relationship and prioritized all the fun a bit more than I probably needed to. By the end of freshman year, it was obvious to me the tradeoff I was making. I was very hard on myself in those early days since I knew the magnitude of the goals I was aiming at and the stakes involved.

Although I had a monumentally successful first year at Penn State, Mr. Garroui's admonition still danced through my mind, "Work hard for the next four years and the rest of your life will be easy." Still, with freshman year behind me, I wasn't just looking forward to summer—I was ready to experience a world beyond everything I'd ever known. **I was headed for Beijing.**

CHALLENGE 4

Bring it Back Out

Go back to the goal or dream that you circled in Challenge 1. My goal to become an aerospace engineer working for NASA seemed ridiculous when I first came up with it. Years later at Penn State, my mental frame matured enough to believe it was truly possible. Take a second look at your goal, what would it look like if you were to pursue it today? Even if your goal still seems out of reach, remember that the path to achieving it is a step-by-step process. What obstacles or fears are keeping you from going after it? Write them down. Is there anything you can do to overcome or mitigate them?

5. CHINA – SCORPIONS ON A STICK

"Travel is fatal to prejudice, bigotry, and narrow-mindedness."
— Mark Twain

By this point in the story, I've already alluded to my early lack of a global perspective relative to some of my peers at Penn State. My worldview was colored by my US centric mindset and upbringing in Pennsylvania. Not having ever traveled outside the country, which is common for people in the US, meant that I was used to a very American way of thinking. This isn't a bad thing in itself, but Mark Twain said it very well. My trip to China would prove to be my most eye-opening experience up to that point. It was full of adventure, new unusual experiences outside my comfort zone, and the development of a truly global perspective.

I had about one week at home between the end of the spring semester and my departure for China. I really had no idea at all what to expect, but I was about as excited as one could possibly be. I had never really packed for a big trip, let alone an entire month away traveling all over China. I eventually fit all the possessions I thought I would need into a single suitcase and a backpack—I would later regret the amount I packed as I lugged them around the country.

The trip began at each student's local airport. When my family dropped me off in Philadelphia, my mom cried her eyes out. The world was a scary place, and China was no exception. At any rate, I had youthful optimism and was already long committed by this point. I met Paul and some of the others at the gate. We made our way first to Toronto, then 7,000 miles across the world to Beijing.

We all arrived at Terminal 3 in Peking airport, which was built for the 2008 Beijing olympics and was itself an engineering marvel. Students were flying in from various U.S. starting points, and so we hung out in the terminal until everyone arrived. It was a fun few hours getting to know the other students as we sat there with Mandarin Chinese playing audibly over the airport PA system.

For several of us, it was our first time out of the United States, and for most, the first time in China. Luckily, the program also brought along a few Penn State international students that were born and raised in China. They'd help us throughout the trip as translators and guides that understood the local culture. Still, our busy agenda meant that we'd visit more cities in 30 days than most Chinese see in their entire lives, so these students were on an experiential adventure just as much as the rest of us.

We eventually made our way to the hotel and the fun began. Despite being physically exhausted from the trip, a few of us stayed up late to hang out and explore the local area. The breakneck pace of the trip and our limited time horizon in China meant that regular sleep was a luxury we simply couldn't afford. Day 2 took us to Tiananmen square, which is sort of like the capital mall behind the White House in Washington, DC.

Our first full day in China involved a trip into the Forbidden City directly in front of Tiananmen square. This was the Emperor's home from the Ming dynasty (1420) to the Qing dynasty (1912). We spent hours exploring the 180 acres of the Forbidden City, making our way progressively deeper and deeper inside. Each section we passed through brought us closer to the Hall of Supreme Harmony, where the Emperor and his court met regularly for momentous occasions. As we would grow accustomed to, a Chinese tour guide accompanied us on our visit to give us the historical background and perspective of everything we were seeing.

As a bunch of Americans, we quickly realized that Chinese breakfast is not quite the same as what we were used to. Professor Wu did his best to put us in hotels that would offer an experience we were a bit more used to, but we still had to adapt to eating marinated hard boiled eggs, congee, and strange sausage links for breakfast. Several of us would go out of our way to master chopsticks, which was a worthy but difficult endeavor. The muscles in our hands started to cramp as we forced them to move in ways they weren't used to several times a day.

By day 3 we were standing at the base of the Great Wall. From our vantage point, it didn't look like what you see on TV. Still, we started our ascent and a group of us ran ahead up the seemingly never ending staircase. The Great Wall is much wider than what I anticipated in most parts, and the sheer size of it was rather impressive. It's hard to believe that the entire thing is over 13,000 miles long, or nearly twice the distance from Beijing to the East Coast of the United States. When we finally reached the peak of the section we were on, we got the picturesque view that many of us had looked up when imagining the trip beforehand. The chinese plains stretched out farther than the eye could see, and the wall along with it. It was a sight to behold, and I stood there realizing this was only the beginning of expanding my perspective beyond the borders of what I had known.

The first few days in China were jaw-dropping. I got to see things that most people I knew back home would only ever see on the TV. As I stood there atop the Great Wall, I pondered how strange that fact was. I found myself there on this journey of a lifetime. It was a lot to take in just then. But I knew it would be my responsibility to soak it all up and report back the sights and experiences to my friends and family upon my arrival back home. It would be my first time acting as some sort of global ambassador, sharing the culture of different people with those back home. I took one long last look out over the plains, realizing it may be the one and only time I ever see them in person. I tried to freeze the mental image in my mind before heading back to the bus.

Back then in 2014, although we all had cell phones, international plans hadn't really become as widespread as they are today. Some of the students had the ability to send text messages, but most of us just used our phones for cameras and as an expensive watch telling us when it was time to meet back up at the bus. Even today, a short 10 years later, the idea of a group of mostly freshmen scattering around in a foreign land with no means of communication is terrifying. Somehow, most of the time, everyone made it back to the bus on time. We did have the occasional lost student, which always gave Xinli quite the scare.

Next up was the Summer Palace on the outskirts of Beijing. The "Long Corridor" (长廊, Cháng Láng, in Mandarin) is a half mile covered walkway ornamented with intricate and beautifully painted woodwork. It's one of the most famous attractions. The summer palace, as its name suggests, was used as a retreat for the Emperor and his family. The large Tower of Buddhist Incense (佛香阁, Fóxiāng Gé) sits up on the hill and overlooks the entire palace area including Kunming Lake (昆明湖, Kūnmíng Hú). The beautiful manmade lake and surrounding forestry made it easy to understand why the Emperor would spend time there.

The first five days in China were an absolute blur. We saw several historical buildings, temples, and monuments that were well known across the world. It was crazy to think that we walked on structures built hundreds or thousands of years before the United States even existed. It was a foreign concept for someone who studied their own history in terms of decades, not centuries or millennia.

By the end of our tour in Beijing, everyone was already exhausted from the long days of adventure and late nights exploring Beijing's nightlife. There was so much to see and so little time to rest. The next city would become my favorite in all of China, and in fact, the whole world.

Next stop– Dalian (大连, Dà Lián).

Dalian is one of China's most famous seaports. We took a flight from Beijing to get there, and I think just about all of us slept every last minute of that flight. That was the name of the game on this trip, squeeze in a catnap wherever you could because we never knew when the next opportunity for rest would come.

As we took the bus from the Dalian International Airport to the city center, it quickly became apparent that we arrived in a place very different from Beijing. The architecture in Dalian was of a more modern style, and the sheer volume of buildings all around us was staggering. Despite it only having one third or one fourth the population density of Beijing, there were high rise apartment buildings as far as the eye could see, and new ones sprouting up in every direction.

We eventually arrived at our hotel and were impressed by a much more lavish experience than what we had in Beijing. It turned out that Xinli's college buddy owned the hotel, and it would be one of the nicer stays during our trip in China. I imagine he heavily subsidized it so Xinli could bring the class there.

This wasn't the first, nor would it be the last, time I was impressed by Dr. Wu's network of friends that spanned not only China but the world. His friendships were a testament to the way he connected with people, and it made me imagine my own future: a life with friends across the globe, each striving to achieve what others consider impossible. I believe there's something powerful about the people you choose to surround yourself with. One of my favorite sayings goes, 'If you hang out with five losers, soon you'll be the sixth.' I like it because the flip side is equally true: if you surround yourself with winners, you'll soon be the sixth.

We were met with extravagance in Dalian, and both the hotel owner and another one of Xinli's friends in the city treated the group to exquisite dinners. The dinners were always a nice reunion for Dr. Wu and his friends, while the rest of us were just happy to be gorging down some seriously out of this world food. Usually when we had one of these formal meals, Xinli would choose a handful of students to sit at the 'VIP' table with him and the hosts. Beyond tasting some of the most amazing seafood I've ever had in my life, we also learned the intricacies of formal Chinese business culture. They taught us how to properly toast and we oftentimes would take turns giving speeches at these events. One of the Chinese students would typically act as a translator between the US and Chinese delegations.

Xinli's second friend in Dalian owned a cigarette manufacturing plant that we were able to tour; it was absolutely massive. Walking in the front door the strong stench of tobacco nearly knocks you off your feet. The CEO showed us how various machines on the assembly line work and answered our basic questions about the volume and scale of their operation. They produced everything from run of the mill cigarettes up to some very high end ones.

The CEO hosted us for dinner in the evening after our tour. Our venue was something out of a Bruce Wayne scene in Batman. In China, it's customary to have all the food on a rotating Lazy Susan type carousell in the middle of the table. Each person has their own plate, and you spin the Lazy Susan with your hand to bring the dish you want a taste of into chopstick attack range. (I say attack because many of us had to fight for our lives to try and grab something as it whizzed by.)

This table, however, was certainly not one you could move with your hand. The table was large enough for our entire group, with more than 35 seats! The room had floor-to-ceiling windows overlooking the ocean, perched high on the edge of a cliff. Looking out over the ocean from Dalian's shore, you could actually see North Korea, which stirred up a mix of emotions.

We wined and dined as we made our customary speeches and toasts. I was often called on for this role—I guess my college public speaking class had paid off. I could quickly switch from a jovial to a very sincere attitude to thank our hosts for their extreme hospitality.

Our adventures in the Chinese seaport unfortunately had come to an end. Our adventure would then take us to Emperor Qinshihuang's ('Chin-shee-hwahng') Mausoleum, in Xian (西安, Xi'An, pronounced 'Shee-an'). In the US at least, this is more famously known as 'The Terracotta Warrior Museum.'

The Terracotta Warriors were discovered accidentally by farmers in 1974, and were originally buried more than 2000 years prior to protect China's first Emperor in the afterlife. The museum has more than 8,000 life-sized warriors, over 500 horses, and 130 chariots. Although certainly not modern, it was most definitely an ancient engineering marvel. Our group was enthralled by the intricate expressions carved into each soldiers' face.

It was mind-boggling to consider humans walking this very same spot 2,000 years earlier. The oldest thing I'd seen up to that point was the Liberty

Bell in Philadelphia, which was just 1/10th the age of the warriors. Although I studied ancient history back in Mountain Top, seeing it first hand gave me a different appreciation for how much life has changed even in the short length of recorded history. It was a lifelong endeavor for many of the artisans, laborers, and craftsmen that built the army.

After things wrapped up in Xian, we would finally find ourselves catching a bit of a break. We were just about half-way into the trip and our next four days would be spent navigating the Yangtze river. Up to this point in my life I had never been on anything bigger than a speedboat, and this ship, although not quite a Carnival cruise ship, was massive. There was a convenience store located on the dock next to the ship, and naturally we took the opportunity to load up on snacks and beverages before climbing aboard. Paul picked up some Chivas Regal Scotch Whiskey. I didn't know what that was, but Paul sure seemed excited about the find.

The next several days would provide us some rest following the breakneck pace from the first two weeks of the trip. As we traveled along the river, we made stops for various daytime excursions. One of my favorite excursions was a trip deep into a ravine on smaller paddle boats. Our tour guides sang traditional songs for us in the local dialect as we cut our way through the mountainous pass.

Although China now has a single unified written language, the spoken language varies immensely from place to place. So much so that Xinli could barely understand people from rural areas such as on this paddle-boat excursion. Once we made our way far enough back, we hopped off the boats onto a floating barge where we'd have a dance party right there in the middle of nowhere, seemingly cut-off from the rest of the world.

I learned a lot of things on this trip in China, but this simple dance party taught me probably one of my most important lessons. Despite coming from wildly different cultures and not being able to communicate a single word to each other, we were all there sharing together in a human experience. I learned that some things, such as dancing and singing, can connect souls with a rapidity that even more direct communication rarely achieves. Looking back now, some of the lessons I learned in China seem obvious, but at that time it felt like a once-in-a-lifetime journey, developing a truly global perspective.

One of the main reasons for taking the river cruise was to pass through the Three Gorges Dam: the largest hydroelectric plant in the world. You might be wondering how you get a boat over a dam; that's a great question. As we found out, the Three Gorges Dam also has the largest ship lock in the world and requires several hours to pass through all five locks. We entered the first lock in the daytime which was a sight to behold. A true modern day engineering marvel. Watching the ship rise at a rate of a few feet per minute eventually became a bit boring, so we headed back under the deck for dinner.

Later in the evening, we surfaced again on the top deck to see the dam from above after leaving the last lock. The dam is about 1.5 miles across and trailed off in the slight fog hanging above the water. We stayed out late on the top deck reminiscing about the trip so far and imagining what was yet to come. The cold night air and little to no moon-light made us wonder how likely it would be for a man overboard to be rescued. As engineering students schooled in probability, we didn't need to ponder it long before deciding we'd rather not find out.

The river cruise was also a great time to really get to know each other. In addition to discussing our thoughts on our present shared experience, we also discussed our collective pasts and our goals and aspirations for the future. The group was pretty young, with a majority of freshmen on the trip. There were some unique goals amongst the group; one guy wanted to be in a rock-band and another wanted to become a teacher.

Paul would ultimately commission in the Marine Corps and fly MV-22 Osprey Tiltrotors all around the world. Then there was me, the guy that wanted to work for NASA. The stars shone brightly that evening, though, and something out in the ether filled me with hope. We would have many great late-night conversations throughout the trip, and for the most part, no dream seemed too crazy to this group. Maybe it was because all of us exploring China together was already crazy enough for anything else to be possible as well.

We finally departed from the river boat in the spice capital of China, Chongqing (重庆). As the story goes, Chongqing has such a high humidity that the local population eats extremely spicy food in an attempt to reduce their susceptibility to the hot temperatures and high humidity. I have no idea if that's true, but one thing is certain—Chongqing is all about spice. Our hotel was built into the side of a rock face adjacent to the river. There was this weird pirate ship thing hanging off the rock face as well. It gave the whole place an odd Pirates of the Caribbean type feel.

The city would become one of my favorite places in all of China, but not for its most famous attraction: the Chongqing Zoo. Despite seeing pandas, giraffes, elephants, and many more exotic animals, my favorite part of the city was actually its cuisine, specifically something called hot pot (火锅 Huǒguō). Hot pot is a Chinese dining style where you have a large boiling pot set in the center of the table. You then order various dishes, typically sliced meat, vegetables, and some seafood. The craziest part of it all, though, is that mostly all raw! You have to pick up the food with your chopsticks and place it into the boiling water to cook it before eating.

Hot pot is one of the most famous dishes in Chongqing, and it's still to this day one of my favorite foods in the entire world. Exploring Chongqing was a great time and an adventurous place to ease our way back into the scene after a few days on the Yangtze River. After successfully stuffing ourselves with hot pot and exploring Chongqing, we were ready for the next part of our journey. Although our next destination was much smaller than the major cities we'd been seeing so far, it would become several students' favorite part of the entire trip. We were going to Professor Wu's childhood village.

Xinli came from a small village of just a few hundred people. I'm not even certain they had electricity or running water when he grew up there. Driving into the village you'd see a stone tablet at the front; etched in the stone are the most famous people from the village and any other honorable people that contributed to its livelihood. Xinli's parents were both involved in the village's governance, so they were on it, and Dr. Wu himself made several large financial donations supporting the village that put his name alongside his parents.

We saw the single barbershop, the single convenience store, the single pharmacy (Chinese herbal medicine), the single elementary school, and that was really about it. It was fascinating to see such a small self-sufficient village. In some regards, comparing it to the major cities we explored earlier on the trip reminded me of my own roots coming from a small-town to now seeing the world. The questions this stirred up were immense. How did Xinli get from this place all the way to State College, Pennsylvania? We would discover the answers to that question bit by bit throughout the trip, and one major key to understanding the mystery was Xinli's family.

Xinli's entire family hosted us for dinner that evening. He had several siblings that still lived close to home, so they came in to prepare the meal for our large group. His childhood home had a very unique layout; there was a sort of middle area in the home that was partially uncovered and exposed the elements. It seemed like a mix between a living room and a sunroom, but we used it as our expanded dining room. We seated ourselves at three large circular tables positioned on the stone floor—luckily it wasn't going to rain that evening.

Chinese culture dictates that an abundance of food should be at the table for guests to leave full. So as per usual we dined for a good two hours. I sat at the table with Xinli, a few other students, and his mom. It was always clear to see how much he cared for his family, particularly his mother. It really made it almost hard to believe at times that he lived on the other side of the world from them. Still, you could sense that being so far away weighed heavily on him.

I guess we all have some difficult life choices to make based on the facts we have and our past experiences. Sometimes, we choose correctly, other times we choose incorrectly. And every so often, the line between the two becomes blurred with a choice that's not so black and white. I've come to realize, though, that choosing one way or the other is always better than avoiding or delaying a hard decision. Despite Xinli living on the other side of the world from his family, he introduced hundreds of Americans to the Chinese people and culture. I credit him with sparking my interest in international affairs, travel, and languages—all of which have led me to become a better, more well-rounded person.

Our last stop on the trip was Shanghai- China's financial capital. If the governing capital of Beijing was like Washington, DC, then Shanghai would be New York City. The Shanghai skyline was transformed over a period of 30 years to be one of the most impressive in the world. Several towering skyscrapers, all located in the same area called 'The Bund,' offer 360-degree views of Shanghai. During our trip, the Shanghai World Financial Center was still under construction, so we went up the second-highest tower, the Pearl TV Tower.

The nighttime view from Pearl Tower was breathtaking. You could see out in every direction for miles on end. The Shanghai city lights glimmered in the distance due to the refraction of the atmosphere over such long distances. Rooftop views of cities would turn out to be one of my favorite things to see while traveling, and starting out with one of the coolest ones in the world was extraordinary.

Our time in Shanghai was jam-packed exploring museums, universities, and doing various other activities around the huge city. Paul and I became friends with one of the street vendor's out front of our hotel. He sold delicious pork buns with a spicy sauce inside. 'Bun man' as we called him, stood on the street all day long and was cheerful every time we saw him, which was 2-3 times a day since we loved the food that much.

Leaving China would be strange. We had such an amazing adventure packed into a very short amount of time. On one hand, I was filled with an immense gratitude and appreciation for having had the opportunity to explore a place so different from where I was born and raised. On the other hand, I was a bit sad knowing it would be quite some time before I'd be able to make it back again, if ever. It was the adventure of a lifetime and each of us knew it. Even if we returned to China someday, we might never again see so deeply into the heart and soul of Chinese culture as we did on this program with Xinli's friends, colleagues, and family.

Speaking of life after China, I had been working on my application to the Schreyer Honors College Gateway program throughout the trip. One of the core pillars of SHC is being a globally engaged citizen. My chance run-in with Professor Wu led me on a one month expedition through the largest cities in China. We interacted with Chinese engineers, American expats, university students, elementary school kids, CEOs, factory workers, and everyday people all across China. For an American, it was the most comprehensive starting point to developing a global perspective I could have ever imagined. I had successfully rounded out the final part of my SHC application.

After initially being rejected as a high school applicant to SHC, an entire year of driving toward a singular focus paid off. From the airport in Shanghai waiting to depart China on the 8,000 mile trip back to the East Coast, **I received an email for admission into the Penn State Schreyer Honors College.**

The many late nights studying calculus, physics, and chemistry in the Penn State stacks had paid off. The past year was the hardest of my life up to this point. I still vividly remember walking out of my way each night in the frigid Pennsylvania winter to get a glimpse of the SHC front entrance and the goal I was chasing. Many nights throughout that very challenging year I wondered if it was all worth it. While my friends were back at the dorms playing video games and doing other things 1st year college students do, I was writing out Taylor series expansions and molecular interactions until they were committed to memory. I found myself in the middle of the scientific process as I tested Mr. Garraoui's hypothesis of hard work paying off in my own life.

In addition to the long hours studying, I added even more financial burden to my family for me to go to China. It was a gamble that this investment in myself would pay-off in the future. Joining SHC, I would return to Penn State in the top 2% of the university. I didn't really know what that would do for me at the time, but the snowball started rolling downhill and it would continue speeding up for several years to come.

As I reflect back on it today, I can't help but feel proud of the efforts and sacrifices of both myself and my family. Although it's healthy to have a balance between work and life, I've never regretted giving it my all at various points along my journey. On the contrary, some of my biggest regrets in life came from times when I gave less than I believed I was capable of.

6. FINDING THE BALANCE

"It is not the mountain we conquer, but ourselves."
— Sir Edmund Hillary

I would wrestle with the sentiment of this quote throughout my second year at Penn State. While pursuing my goals, several obstacles would be placed in my way. And I even placed some of them there. I correlated action with success, which led me to sign up for more than I could handle at the time. Throughout the year I would learn that focused action, rather than motion alone, is the major determining factor between success and failure. I learned this lesson very painfully after pushing myself to the brink.

On my return to the US, I had a single week back home with my friends and family before I was to report back to Penn State for my summer research opportunity in the aerospace department. The deal I made with Professor Smith—to earn a 4.0 in my first semester—secured me a summer slot in Penn State's Vertical Lift Research Center of Excellence (VLRCOE). My time at home was a nice break despite the chaos of running around seeing all my family. I recounted my adventure in China and caught up on some much needed sleep. My time at home quickly came to an end, and although I didn't realize it at the time, those short visits would become the new normal as I leaned further into school and the relentless pursuit of my goals.

I arrived at Penn State and moved into a shared apartment in downtown State College. Although Penn State's climate was frigid during much of the school year, the summers were rather hot and sticky. My apartment was a three floor townhome with a basement and several bedrooms that I shared with a few other students staying at Penn State for the summer. I split a room with Pat from my freshman dorm. He was studying electrical engineering and, to this day, remains one of the smartest people I've ever met. Like me, Pat was pursuing a summer research opportunity. The other housemates were random people we found on Craigslist.

I took a desk in the VLRCOE. All the other students there were pursuing Masters or PhD degrees, so it was a bit odd for me to be there as a freshman. I was placed next to an MS student who would be my mentor for the summer. My initial job was to study engineering textbooks on helicopter design and analysis. The material was complex and far beyond my current comprehension. I felt like I was drinking from a firehose with an overwhelming amount of information coming at once. I also would print out conference and journal papers of whatever I thought was relevant. The math and physics in those papers was well beyond my current level, which meant I could spend a few hours reading a 15 page research paper and still only understand the introduction. This was my daily routine early on.

Summer in State College is immensely fun. Although we were busy, Pat and I got into our fair share of shenanigans. I don't know what possessed him to do it, but Pat was dead set on brewing his own beer. We (really Pat, but I was along for the ride) bought all the equipment needed to make your own mash on top of the stove, distill it, and get it into a carboy container. We made a 5-gallon batch early in the summer that would have to sit in the cool basement for a few weeks before being ready to try.

We also hosted a few house parties in the apartment. One of my good friends was a DJ, and another collected payment at the door. Even after paying our 'employees' and our expenses, we managed to turn a profit. It was my first taste of entrepreneurship, and though I thought it was neat that we made money, I didn't dwell on it much. I focused more on doing well in the research position and managing family matters back home.

Early that summer, I received the news that my grandfather was in the hospital, not doing well, and that I should come home to see him. I sped about 95 miles per hour the entire two-and-a-half hours home where I found him tied up to all sorts of machines in the hospital—it was reminiscent of a scene not yet buried deep enough in my memory. We had seen my mom in the hospital just a few years earlier, but this felt different. He was old and ailing from severe health issues caused by a life of smoking and alcohol abuse. They eventually released him from the hospital so he could go home and be more comfortable in his final days—his body was beginning to fail him on a major scale.

Over the next two or three weeks, I would go through this cycle of driving back to Penn State to work a few days before getting an emergency phone call and having to drive home. I was distracted at work thinking about home, and distracted at home thinking about work. It was a tough few weeks. The travel was getting to be a bit too much and I had to decide whether or not I would drive in each time the phone rang. One night, my mom and aunt called me together, which was a bad sign that my mom couldn't make the phone call by herself. My aunt, who was the oldest of six, was gentle yet matter of fact, "You better come home—we think it's time."

It was important for me to be there. I had gone off to school and my pursuits had taken me around the world. Life is funny though—no matter how important we consider our jobs, our careers, and a number of other things we fill our days with, relationships with those we care about are what really matter. Having had four elder grandparents when I left for China, I knew there was a possibility for something like this to happen while I was gone. Luckily, I was now just two hours away instead of half the world away.

I sat with my family at my grandfather's bedside for a few hours that evening as we reminisced on old stories. This side of my family had always been extremely close. Both my mother and father were one of six children, and we had a lot of cousins on my mom's side as well. We all basically grew up together, and a lot of them were there at my grandfather's house that night.

Although they all followed different, difficult, twisting paths to get there, my mother, my aunt, and my uncle were all in the medical field. The kids (my siblings, my cousins, and I) had grown used to hearing whispers as the adults discussed my grandfather's condition. You didn't have to be in the medical field, though, to see what was coming.

That evening, my grandfather would pass away as we all sat by his side. My mom and her siblings were all religious to some extent, and regardless of what everyone in the room believed, leaning on some faith seemed like a pretty good choice at the time. We sang some of my grandparents' favorite hymns, crowded together in the room around him.

The whole process was slow. I was sitting close to him and held his hand during his final minutes. Eventually, my aunt came over and checked his pulse—he was gone. It was the first time I'd see someone die right before my own eyes. All my mom's siblings, the real adults in the room, were immediately reduced to a complete mess. They didn't exactly have the best relationship with their father growing up, but obviously the death of a parent is something that weighs heavy on anyone.

I comforted my younger cousin who was sitting next to me sobbing as I tried to hold back my own tears. Of everyone there, I somehow became the strong one, simply because someone had to. In life we are sometimes called to action and meet the expectations set for us, while other times we exceed them. I'm proud looking back remembering I was able to be there for my family when they needed me most. I grew up a lot in those short few weeks. This was the first time, but certainly not the last, that I would face such an emotionally daunting experience.

With this weight of family loss still lingering, I returned to the routines and demands at Penn State, but with a new perspective on what really mattered. I remember being very grateful for Dr. Smith, who was extremely understanding of the situation. It was a tough summer, but one that pushed me to expand both mentally and emotionally. It would serve as a good reminder that no matter how busy life gets, you should never allow trivial things to get in the way of relationships with those you care about most. There wouldn't be much more time to reflect, though, as my second year at Penn State was about to begin.

My sophomore year at Penn State leaned more towards aerospace engineering. A mix of pre-engineering courses, calculus 4, quantum physics, and thermodynamics was enough to keep me busy. I did manage getting into two aerospace courses, which was rare for students before junior year. Having the SHC name now behind me would help many times with getting into full classes.

One of the aerospace courses was called Flight Vehicle Design and Fabrication, but we all just called it *Sailplane* because the instructor pioneered airplane winglet technology that you now find standard on most airplanes. That class exposed us to basic airplane design and also had a lab component where we could put the equations we learned in the classroom to practice. The lab was a sort of maker space with various teams in the class working on different projects. The other aerospace class I took was a special elective on wind energy engineering. This was another project based course where another friend from freshman year, Mitch, and I were building an 18 inch diameter wind turbine to compete in the Department of Energy's Collegiate Wind Competition (CWC).

Both Sailplane and the CWC activities had students ranging from freshman through seniors, which was an ideal learning opportunity for younger students like me and Mitch. My schedule was extremely demanding as I tried to balance these intense classes with my continually expanding social life at Penn State.

I had started hanging out at the fraternities a lot in the spring semester of my freshman year. This fall I found a house that seemed like a really good fit for me and decided to join. It was a fun group of guys that I could see myself getting along with, and a handful of rather studious ones as well. Notably, two guys that joined the year before as freshman were in my same aerospace pre-major classes, which gave me some confidence that it was possible to have this type of college experience and be serious about school.

I volunteered to be Pledge Class President for my group of 24 new recruits since I thought it would look good on my resume. That meant that any time anyone needed anything, whether a brother or a fellow pledge, it typically went through me. Pledging responsibilities on top of demanding coursework were crushing. This was another example of signing up for more things than I should have **because I mistook motion for achievement.**

A large part of pledging were pointless things like calisthenics in the basement during the freezing Penn State winter. This was meant to bond the group together, sharing a mutual experience that was unique to that group alone. All of this was fine—I actually considered it a good workout since I didn't otherwise make time to exercise. The real challenge was the time commitment of all the frat-related activities. We were also responsible for maintaining the house, working parties almost every night of the week, and pretty much handling any and all of the grunt work.

I found myself struggling to balance my course work with the demands of pledging and the other extra-curricular activities I was involved in such as the wind competition. Between my responsibilities to the house and my classes, there wasn't much time for sleep. I was usually at the house until around three in the morning, often having to be back by six AM. I often slept on the couch to catch a few extra minutes of sleep by cutting out my commute time. Clearly, I wasn't getting enough sleep at night. This resulted in me sleeping in class on more than one occasion, with Sal or one of the other guys giving me a jab if I started to snore so I wouldn't disrupt the class.

At the same time I was pledging, my relationship with my brother continued to deteriorate. To me it seemed that he hadn't taken his academic studies too seriously and was more interested in partying. I saw firsthand what happens when you don't wisely set your priorities. I realize the irony of that statement after just describing how I caught up on sleep in class. Still, my perspective on the situation meant that I put a lot of pressure on myself to succeed so that I'd be in a position to take care of my family someday.

This made it very difficult for me when just two weeks before final exams,

I majorly bombed an engineering test. It was probably the worst grade I ever got in my life; something like a 48%, which was simply unacceptable to me. It became clear that I swung the pendulum too far.

I initially wanted to join a fraternity for the social aspects and group of friends I would be making, but it seemed I was sacrificing too much in the process. I didn't know it at the time, but I was considering quitting on our very last day of pledging. The fraternity's president somehow reassured me that everything would work out fine and I decided to stay. That next day we finished pledging and I went into hiding in the library for two straight weeks in an attempt to salvage my grades. I'd have to score 20-30% higher than my performance up to that point in the semester just to maintain a B-average in my classes.

Somehow, I managed to pull off a few last-minute miracles. In reality, my other friends in aerospace played a large role helping me get back up to speed on the material that would be on our finals. I ended the semester with a much lower GPA than my first two. I called my mom to tell her how I'd done. There was silence on the other end of the phone for a few moments. She asked a very simple yet piercing question, "Are you happy with that?" I could hear the disappointment in her voice—a rare moment that stung deeply. My entire family knew I had what it took to be successful at school, and serious sacrifices were made to give me the opportunity to be there. Hearing the disappointment from my mom was just about the most severe yet effective punishment the world could have delivered me for my poor performance.

Although the grades were less than what I aimed for, I still did comparatively well for someone pledging. The soft skills I gained in the frat would prove invaluable throughout my life. It transformed me from a nerdy annoying kid to a social chameleon good at interacting with different types of people.

Internally I always had an immense appreciation for the set of skills Greek life afforded me, but only through the process of writing this book have I been pressed to concisely state what those skills are. I learned how to synthesize vast amounts of seemingly unrelated inputs to create actionable plans for achieving a common goal. I learned how to divide and delegate tasks among a group of sleep-deprived college students with more important things they'd rather be doing. I became a master at adjusting my speech and my demeanor to match my environment and the people I was talking to.

The fraternity taught me many skills in leadership, ownership and accountability, and how to deal with people. It was a master class in some very important life skills that would serve me well for years to come. I'd still have to learn how to apply these skills to my studies and career as I continued searching for the elusive work-life balance. As with several other challenging things I've done over the years, I would almost immediately see the payoff of my hard work.

Over the winter break I flew to Dallas Fort-Worth in Texas for the Bell Helicopter Boot Camp. Twenty students from around the country arrived at the Bell Headquarters to participate in the week-long engineering activity. It was an intensive experience where two teams of 10 engineering students were to design a solution to a Bell relevant engineering problem. All week long we learned from engineers throughout the company as they simultaneously evaluated each of us and tried to convey that Bell was the place to be. It was an intense process with long, jam-packed days.

My expertise in modeling aircraft components in the computer, which I had done much of already at Penn State, allowed me to help my team visualize the solutions we developed. I made some lifelong friends that week as we worked around the clock to come up with the best solution. It came as a surprise to me at the time that our biggest challenge wasn't technical at all—it was interpersonal. The group had several smart individuals from various backgrounds and skill levels. The high pressure situation, which was arguably a major objective of the boot camp, exposed and exacerbated weaknesses throughout the team.

I attempted to apply my new skills from the fraternity to smooth things over where I could, but learned I was ill-equipped to handle differences of opinion on multiple seemingly well thought out paths forward. We luckily had a much older student, who had previously served time in the military. He stepped up to be the wiser team member we needed to keep the team working well together and I jumped in to help steer the overarching technical approach. Our entire team came together to achieve victory. Our prize for winning was a helicopter ride over the Dallas Cowboys football stadium; it was my first time flying in a helicopter.

The experience was an unbelievable introduction to real-world applied engineering, and affirmed that I was on an interesting path with my studies and rotorcraft focus at Penn State. Many of the boot campers from both teams were extended offers to return for a summer internship. One of our team members that caused many of the interpersonal issues was not invited to return. It was a powerful lesson for me: you don't get far in life by being a jerk, no matter how smart you are.

I found my time at Bell extremely rewarding. It confirmed my belief that there was more to being a successful engineer than simply being smart or talented. **To be truly effective, one must balance their technical ability with extraordinary communication skills.** There was obviously a lot for me to learn at Bell, both technical and in life, so I accepted an offer with their rotor stress analysis group and would return to Texas in the summer for a much longer 10 week internship. Things felt like they were falling into place.

Back at Penn State I locked in for the spring semester which was a continuation of my difficult course list from the fall. I had some making up to do for the prior semester, and I re-visited some of my freshman year study habits to get the job done. I mostly lived in the library and at various other study spots from Sunday through Friday. On Friday evening, I'd study until 9 or 10 pm and then walk directly over to the fraternity for whatever party we had going on that night. I was only at the house on evenings over the weekend, which was the requisite back-swing of the pendulum to set me on a good track again in school.

In addition to my demanding coursework, I continued to pursue a few extra-curricular activities. One such excursion was an SHC visit to the Naval Academy in Annapolis, Maryland. It was the first time I'd meet Marine General, former Astronaut, and NASA Administrator Charles Bolden in person. I never could have guessed it at the time, but our paths would cross more than once in years to come.

I closely kept watch for easy-to-miss opportunities that came through my email such as this trip to Annapolis. Oftentimes, it seemed my engineering classmates didn't understand why I took on all these extra efforts. And although they further added to the complexity of my daily schedule, I learned a lot by interacting with people from various backgrounds and walks of life. In fact, I would go as far as to say some of these activities were more instrumental to my learning and development than an entire 16-week engineering course. I still wasn't doing it perfectly, but I was starting to figure out the difference between being busy and being focused. I was learning to properly channel my energy toward a consistent aim.

Throughout the semester I also continually applied to various national fellowships and NASA internships. I figured I had an interesting story and decided to put my name in the running. Rejection came swiftly on all fronts. I didn't receive the prestigious fellowships and I never heard back on my NASA application. But I didn't take it too personally since I was still a young student at Penn State. Surely someday I would be a good applicant for these types of prestigious national awards.

Despite those rejections, I finished the semester strong and successfully demonstrated to myself that I could find a balance between academics and an intense social life. By pretty much anyone's standards, even my own, I made a full recovery from the abomination of my academic performance during pledging. Now it was time to apply my new knowledge and skills in the real world; I was off to Texas for a 10 week summer internship at Bell Helicopter.

7. TEXAS – HONEY BUTTER CHICKEN BISCUITS

"You have brains in your head. You have feet in your shoes. You can steer yourself any direction you choose."

— Dr. Seuss

Sometimes in life we're faced with difficult choices. This quote reminds me that even when we come to a fork in the road, we have the capacity within ourselves to make a good decision. This chapter describes my first real aerospace engineering work experience outside of Penn State. The internship was so amazing that I started to consider what a career there would look like. An alternate path from the one I originally envisioned had formed, and I would soon have to decide which road to follow.

Euless, TX, June 2015.

The alarm rang out at 5 AM, as it did most days during the summer of 2015. It was the classic iPhone alarm that sounds like a bomb is about to go off; it's enough to wake you out of even the deepest sleep. I was sharing an apartment with another one of the Bell Helicopter interns, Connor. We both participated in the Bell Boot Camp a few months prior, and were now working as engineers in the Bell headquarters building.

Connor and I held to a rigorous schedule during the week. The wakeup call came at 5 AM, though Connor usually wouldn't roll into action until closer to 5:30. We'd grab some quick showers, prep our lunches for the day and our gym bags for after work, put on some nice business casual attire and we'd be off. Connor usually wore a polo, while I preferred a button-down.

A Houston native, Connor had a strong Texas accent. He also had the coolest car of the entire group of over a hundred interns. It was his grandfather's 1966 green Ford mustang. The thing was a real gem and quite a good looking classic. The only problem was that it didn't have air conditioning. Coincidentally, it also didn't have airbags, but we accepted the risk partially to look cool, partially because that was our only option. Luckily one of the perks of heading to work at six in the morning is that it was usually still a cool 80 degrees outside, almost not hot enough to break a sweat.

Bell's headquarters was situated in Euless, which is about halfway between the two major Texas cities Dallas and Fort Worth. Dallas was the more modern area with a financial district, the Cowboys stadium, and what I thought of more as a city vibe. Fort Worth was the total opposite; the main attraction was the Stock Yards, where you could go see a live rodeo with cowboys, cowboy hats and boots, and bulls.

We had two other roommates during the summer, and all four of us lived in a very convenient apartment complex just behind the Headquarters building. It was far enough that we'd still drive over most days, especially given the repercussions of walking outside for more than 3 minutes in the Texas heat.

I was in the rotor design and analysis group at Bell, which did structural analysis for the company's various helicopters. Throughout the summer, I'd work on both commercial and military platforms.

Most of my work involved running computer models to test if the rotor parts could handle the expected forces without failing. My favorite aspect of the work was when I got to use Bell's computing clusters, which you can think of as several dozen computers strung together into a very large and powerful one.

Connor was in a different group, but we still found ways to get into mischief around Bell. He was a very hands on kind of guy, a grease-monkey, and really enjoyed talking shop. I eventually found the flight line, but the only problem was that I wore a button down and tie most days. Even coming from a more rural part of Pennsylvania, I looked too much the part of a snooty engineer and wasn't immediately welcomed into the mechanics' world. Connor on the other hand was a natural, he'd walk right up to them and say some funny Texan stuff with his Houston accent. They'd laugh over whatever it was while I stood there just trying to decipher all the slang and strange phrases being thrown around me. Our skill sets were complementary and we made a good duo.

We eventually became friends with Bert; he was in charge of maintaining all the helicopters that operated out of the HQ flight line. Bert was a riot to talk to and was happy to tell me and Connor all about the various helicopters. He told us what the engineers had done well, and also showed us where they had engineered something that made the aircraft extremely difficult to maintain or repair. Out of the entire group of interns, I'm nearly certain we were the only ones getting this level of practical and well-rounded experience. Knowing the difference between something that could be designed in the computer or on paper and something that could be made in real life is probably one of the most valuable engineering skills I've ever picked up. And it was initially thanks to Bert and his lessons.

Every so often, one of the helicopters would be going up for a routine flight for one reason or another. "You guys wouldn't want to jump in now, would ya?" Bert asked. Two 20 year olds were certainly not saying no to helicopter rides. Throughout the summer, we flew in several different Bell models including the historic Bell 47, made famous from the TV show *MASH* for its role in the Vietnam war.

My work was challenging, but also great fun. My mentor did a great job balancing some of the more tedious work with projects that would excite me and allow me to really wrap my head around a problem. The exciting design work helped me power through some of the more tedious tasks. Still, it was clear that I poured my heart and soul into the design work that I found most interesting. I was seeing Steve Jobs' observation about doing what you love play out in my own life.

Bell had to be pretty strict with tracking hours spent on each project to bill the government and other funding sources properly. This meant that employees had to track their time down to the sixth of an hour, even the interns.

Had it not been for their rule of interns not going over 40 hours per week, I would have most certainly done so to soak up all the experience that I could. Still, not having the option to stay longer forced us to get out and explore the DFW metropolitan area.

Connor and I, along with some of the other interns, would often go exploring the night scenes in both Dallas and Fort Worth. They were about equidistant from Bell, but something about Fort Worth made it feel closer. Maybe it was that culturally it felt more of what I expected out of Texas. It's like when we were in Fort Worth, we were on a continuous adventure looking back into a storied Texas past. We saw the rodeo, learned line dancing, ate some of the best steak I've ever had in my life, and had an all around amazing time.

As part of our rigorous schedule, Connor and I often went to the gym directly from work. It was a sight to behold as we exited the Bell HQ front doors, and immediately started unbuttoning our dress shirts in an attempt to delay the sweating. The sweltering Texas heat turned Bell's large asphalt parking lot into a sauna in the afternoons.

By the time we made the less than 100 foot walk to the car, we were already dripping. Getting to the car was one thing, getting in was a whole different story. The 66' Mustang had leather seats and metallic seatbelts. You can imagine what black leather scorched by the Texas sun all day would feel like. Once we were seated, we had to rapidly tap the metal seat belt clips to slowly dissipate some of the heat, or numb our hands, I guess I'm not too sure which one it really was. After a bit of a struggle along with some profanities, we were buckled up and ready to go. Without airbags, it seemed seat belts were the least we could do.

The gym was a good 15 minutes from Bell, and we had ourselves a time there. Connor and I were pretty good at pushing each other by delivering repeated insults every time one of us was visibly slacking. We were two skinny guys at the time; but we gained a good bit of muscle over the ten-week internship.

By the time we finished up at the gym and made it back home, there was only an hour or two left of the day. I'd often be found by the pool working on something on my laptop. The schedule was intense but I had satisfaction from the rapid growth I was making at work, in the gym, and in my headspace. I wanted to be sure that if I ever looked back on it, I would be happy with the effort I put in. We certainly had our fun in Texas, but I was there on a mission to gain real-world experience, and continue marching toward my goals.

Speaking of my goals and future plans, another great part of the internship was my working relationship with both my direct mentor and my division supervisor. My mentor was in the cubicle directly next to me. This made it extremely easy, likely too easy, for me to pop over with all sorts of questions throughout the day. He taught me so much that summer about structural analysis, designing with manufacturing in mind, computer modeling, and the general inner workings of a place like Bell. He always seemed to have the answers and almost never seemed annoyed or too busy for my questions.

My division supervisor was actually the technical recruiter that picked me out from the twenty students at the Bell Boot Camp. We would meet once every other week for the duration of the summer; we called them one-on-ones. I came to really look forward to these tag-ups. My supervisor was a straight shooter, incredibly nice, and full of wisdom to share.

One day I asked him about the book-shelf behind him, "What kinds of books are you into?" He thought about it for a second and replied, "Mostly self-help books." "Self help?" I asked. I still wasn't much of a reader at the time, but his simple comment set me in motion. I picked up a book titled "See You at the Top" by Zig Ziglar and read it by the apartment complex pool for the next several weeks. I was a painfully slow reader at the time, often getting distracted and having to read the same passage several times to internalize the meaning behind the words I was subvocalizing. Although it took weeks to get through it, that one book would lead me on an extraordinary journey of personal discovery and growth.

My supervisor might have regretted this because I started asking him some harder life questions, "How do we know whether or not the grass is greener on the other side?" It was obvious I was asking in the context of taking a job at Bell vs. pursuing a career elsewhere. In other words, for my particular situation, it was Bell versus NASA. He replied in a very fair and honest way, concluding that if one was happy where they were at, then it doesn't matter what color the grass is on the other side of the fence. This seemed like a prophetic response at the time, but I was still tempted to peek over the fence and find out for myself. Looking back, those sessions were invaluable in shaping not only my career but also my approach to personal growth.

This summer at Bell was going to be my last application to NASA. I had already applied every semester since starting at Penn State and didn't hear back a single time. It's not that I lost hope, but rather that I found another great option right there in front of me. So I made a deal with myself: I would put in one final application to NASA. If I didn't get in this time, then I'd graduate with my bachelor's degree, move to Texas, and climb the ladder at Bell. It seemed like an amazing outcome for how hard I'd been working and would lead to many exciting career opportunities.

I hadn't given up on working at NASA, but the reality of the situation set in and my rational mind decided that a future in Texas was a great choice. Still, I was going to make sure this final NASA application was the best one yet. Remember, I only regretted failing when I knew I hadn't tried my best. Although it would still take me a few years to develop this mindset, I now believe that if you try your absolute best, you cannot fail. Back in the summer of '15 at Bell, however, failing to get into NASA was still very much on the table.

But I now had experience in one of the country's top helicopter engineering academic programs and one of the leading helicopter manufacturing companies. My experiences covered a huge spectrum including structural analysis, aerodynamic design, high performance computing, and even building models and flight testing them. I was deeply involved in a diverse set of activities across Penn State's campus with both social and professional organizations, and I even co-founded an aerospace club in my sophomore year at Penn State. My technical abilities were impressive, but as I learned in the fraternity, it didn't mean anything if you couldn't properly convey them.

To this end, I remember writing an entire essay to answer every single question on the application. I answered a simple question like 'When did you graduate highschool?' with a three-paragraph essay about my desire to work for NASA from a young age. I wrote more in those few weeks preparing that application than I probably had in my entire life up to that point. I really don't consider myself to be an author, and definitely not a creative writer. I'm also certain that back then my writing was far worse than it is now.

There was a little community pool in our apartment complex that I'd sit by many evenings typing away on my laptop. The Texas heat kept it warm outside pretty much all night long; so I could sit there as long as was needed to struggle through the essays. I sent many of them back to Penn State contacts in the University Fellowships Office, who helped me revise and rewrite them multiple times.

I also had a few friends who were more acquainted with the complex art of written English. And I solicited their feedback on the more important essays. Megan was one of those people who I'd reach out to from time to time for feedback on my writing. She was into reading just like my brother Ryan—both book worms through and through. One of the administrative assistants at Bell was also extremely generous to give me feedback on parts of the application. She knew I would do great at Bell, but she was also excited for the prospect of me following my dream to work for NASA.

After what seemed like an eternity, I was finally ready to send the application into the abyss. I hit 'submit' and it felt like a big weight lifted off my shoulders. That was the best application I could have put forward. If I never heard back, I would be quite content with the effort I put in.

Friedrich Nietzsche wrote, "And if you gaze long enough into an abyss, the abyss will gaze back into you." I had been on my journey to work at NASA for about 7 years by this point. I was ready to move on. Setting that goal seven years earlier to work for NASA and seriously pursuing it was still one of the greatest choices I ever made. Even if I never made it to NASA, the person I became through the process was someone I could be proud of for the rest of my days. Still, I wouldn't know one way or the other for several months.

With the application submitted, it was time to focus on finishing out a great internship at Bell. The work during my time there was both challenging and engaging. It was clear the company had some of the world's brightest helicopter engineers.

Another good mentor was Dr. Al Brand. He got his PhD in aerospace engineering from Georgia Tech, which is another one of the three major rotorcraft engineering schools in the US along with Penn State and the University of Maryland. Al was one of the company's leading engineers for rotor aerodynamics—the study of how the rotor lifts the helicopter. He had published ground-breaking work increasing our understanding of a phenomenon that plagued helicopters for many years. In the helicopter aerodynamics world, Al was a bit famous.

I didn't work with Al on any projects that summer. But he taught a class for the interns called 'Introduction to Helicopter Aerodynamics.' One day I caught him in the hallway. We were standing next to the fish bowl, which was this odd shaped conference room in the middle of the building with floor to ceiling glass walls—so everyone walking by could see inside. We chatted for a few minutes and he asked me, "What are you thinking of doing after you graduate?" I have to believe it was mostly a rhetorical question, because he then very clearly explained to me the benefits of getting a PhD. To drive his point home he said, "plus it would be cool to have a 'Dr.' in front of your name." Seemed like a good enough reason to me.

I had certainly considered graduate school before that point, thanks to my summer research in the VLRCOE and several discussions with Professor Smith. Still, I was on the fence about it. I knew the alternative was to graduate in about a year, start working, and finally begin helping my family out financially. Al's pitch somehow made it seem like a much more attractive choice. But that decision would still be at least another year or two away.

As the summer drew to a close, I worked up until the last minute to close out my project. Connor and I, along with some of the others, did one last outing to Whataburger. We ventured there many times throughout the summer late at night since it was one of the only places that would still be open. Almost every time we'd get the same thing—Honey Butter Chicken Biscuits and their entirely too large chocolate milkshake. Texas sure knew how to make some tasty food. We'd reminisce on the events that unfolded around us throughout the summer including our several helicopter rides, the cool adventures throughout Dallas Fort Worth, and the fascinating projects that the majority of us worked on.

I realized too late in life the importance of the friendships made during these short-term experiences. Our intern groups would often fall quickly out of touch as we re-located all across the country. I was sad to lose my friends the first few times, but eventually it became a bit more normal for me, or at least something I grew accustomed to. I would keep in touch with a handful from each experience, including Connor, but the overwhelming majority of my fellow interns I would never see again. Still, the lessons and perspectives I developed over the ten weeks in a mutual experience with them, along with all the others at Bell, helped shape me into who I am today.

One additional thought I have reflecting on my time at Bell is the importance of finding good mentors. I've come to realize that mentors aren't always senior professionals; they're anyone who can teach you something valuable. If we're honest with ourselves, the majority of people out there could mentor us in one thing or another. I found many great mentors at Bell, and several of them had a positive influence on my future for years to come.

Before leaving Texas, I was offered a return position for the following summer in Al's group: *Flight Technology Research and Development*. Coincidentally, or maybe not, it seemed to have the highest concentration of advanced degree holding folks in the company. I gladly accepted and was relieved that life was starting to take on some semblance of consistency. All good things must eventually come to an end, though, and this was no different. It was time to return to Penn State, for what we all knew would be the hardest semester of our lives.

While writing this book, a friend shared the best answer I've ever heard to the question I posed to my supervisor midway through summer '15 at Bell: "The grass is greener where you water it." In the end, I learned that things generally work out, no matter which path we choose at a fork in the road. The key is to commit to the path you've chosen and keep nurturing it along the way.

CHALLENGE 5

Envision the Future

Is the grass greener on the other side? When you go after a goal one of two things can happen: either you don't attain the goal, or you succeed. In case 1, you learn from your mistakes and can attack it again smarter and better if you so choose. In case 2, you actually succeed. Let's assume for a moment that achieving your goal is just a matter of repeating the above process until you succeed. What would your life look like if you did so? I encourage you to write that out a bit below. Write about a typical day in the life you envision. What would you do, see, and feel?

8. THE HARDEST SEMESTER OF YOUR LIFE

"Success is not final, failure is not fatal: It is the courage to continue that counts."

— Winston Churchill

There were several times in my journey when I felt like I was losing the good fight. Often, this was because I took on too much and struggled to stay afloat under the weight of all my responsibilities. At times, I felt as if I was letting not only myself down but also those around me. This quote from Churchill reminded me that even our biggest perceived failures don't have to define our future. **No matter where we are, it's our next move that truly counts.**

At Penn State's New Student Orientation, we heard the warning: 'Only one in five of you will cross the stage at graduation.' Aerospace engineering was keeping up with its promise. Junior year at Penn State is when the true aerospace curriculum begins in earnest. To get into those classes you needed to maintain a minimum GPA of 3.0.

I was always confused how one could get below a 3.0 GPA. Even in my most challenging semester while pledging, I stayed above that. That statement will probably make a lot of people angry, but it's the truth. I worked my butt off in school, and anything less than an A was unacceptable to me. Whether for lack of trying, external factors outside their control, or simply not being able to grasp the material quickly enough, many aerospace pre-major students had already switched to other majors. By this point, we probably weren't too far off the one in five metric.

Still, things were only getting harder. Our fall schedule consisted of a crash course in aerospace topics ranging from literal rocket science to advanced mathematics. On top of all that, I was taking the same Sailplane class I took since Freshman year, an independent research class to work on the wind turbine competition, and nutrition. This was 17 credits whereas most students were only taking 12-15.

I'll never forget the first day of classes—one of our first was aerodynamics. A young German Professor, Sven, would teach us how fluid flows around weirdly shaped objects for the next four months. On the first day, however, he had a bit of a warning for us when he said, "The next four months will be the hardest semester of your life." Despite his warning, the atmosphere in the room was energetic. We finally made it to the real aerospace classes. Still, there was something slightly unnerving about what Sven had just told us.

Deep down we all already knew this, but being warned by a professor about it on the first day of class underscored the fact that it was a very serious matter. The reality of the situation was that if you start to slip in any one of the classes, you'd enter a downward spiral that would be nearly impossible to recover from.

On top of my classwork, I was also still competing in the Collegiate Wind Competition (CWC). My friend Mitch and I took a Wind Energy Engineering class the previous year, competing in the second Annual Department of Energy competition to get our feet wet. We realized we needed a club format to build long-term expertise and become dominant over the long run.

Mitch led the electric generator development, for which the team hand wound custom designed motors (a complex, time-consuming process). The task was painstakingly laborious, with hundreds if not thousands of copper coil windings going into a single motor assembly. The rows needed precise alignment to prevent performance losses.

As for me, I was the aerodynamics lead and our sub-team's main priority was the rotor aerodynamic design. We designed improved wind turbine rotor blades that we then 3D printed. My other major contribution was a mechanism that allowed us to actively move the blades during their operation. I knew from my time in the VLRCOE and at Bell that moving the blades would give the best performance across all wind speeds, which would be crucial for doing well in the competition. We tested many motor and rotor combinations in the aerospace building's wind tunnel throughout the semester. It was great having our own tunnel downstairs because it allowed us to rapidly try, fail, and try again. The tunnel filled a massive room, and we crowded around the reinforced windows watching the turbine in action.

At the same time I was leading the CWC team, I was also a team lead for the Design Build Fly (DBF) competition in the Sailplane class. The course has two main projects and I gravitated towards the one with a much faster pace. We built, tested, failed, and then built it better. I was quickly learning the value of this fast iteration approach—aiming to quickly fail so that we could learn and improve the design. Sal was the other DBF co-lead and was the structural lead for the airplane. He was responsible for our aircraft being strong enough to fly. We were both on the team the year prior, but our aircraft had a serious vibration problem limiting the speed at which we could fly. Sal's job was to make sure that didn't happen again this year.

My role was again as aerodynamics lead. It was my job to size the airplane (pick its major dimensions such as the size of the wing and fuselage.) The hardest part of all this was the time required to physically build the aircraft.

The sailplane lab overlooked the courtyard next to the aerospace building. It was on the third floor and had a mix of scents: epoxy glue, balsa wood, and burnt plastic. Long hours would be spent cutting strips of balsa and assembling them together with epoxy to make the wing. I remember I once rushed through the wing build—I mean hey, it was the hardest semester of our lives after all. Sal took one look at it and said very matter of factly, "We can't use this." I was peeved since even a subpar wing took hours to make. After some careful thinking, we began laser cutting the balsa wood parts that would be used to construct the wing. This created some consistency in the manufacturing process.

Eventually we got a good wing, and then it was my job to wrap it tightly in thin plastic to transform it from a skeleton to what looked like a real wing. The aircraft design was a bit janky. We'd get extra points at the competition for a compact design so we built hinges into the wing. All these complexities made for a challenging design, and Sal and I were both equally booked with extremely busy schedules. It was tough finding the hours needed to be in the lab working on the plane. We'd often find ourselves working late into the night on whatever the particular challenge of the day happened to be.

These competition teams were immensely valuable to me even though they added extra work to my schedule. I was able to take the equations being learned in the classroom and put them to the test, thus learning how they worked in practice. It was a challenge to squeeze them in on top of the demanding courses we were taking, but that wasn't all that I was trying to balance.

I constantly worked to blend my aerospace activities with a social life at Penn State. Sal, myself, and our other engineering friends all still enjoyed having a good time on the weekends. We were definitely in the rowdier crowd and, in a strange twist of events, had somehow become the 'cool kids.' One of the most important items on our social calendar was Penn State football.

The football season resulted in us losing 7 entire Saturdays in the fall semester. Fans from all over the country travel in for the game, or tailgating at least. Tailgating is a sacred activity at Penn State where more than one hundred thousand people fill several acres of fields surrounding the stadium before the game. Most people go into the game then, but some come all the way to the middle of nowhere Pennsylvania just to tailgate. We almost always went into the game unless someone partied too hard at the tailgate and had to be taken home. That was a big party foul, but it did happen. So we'd start partying around 8 AM, and go straight through the night until 2 AM. It was a marathon that we ran as if it was a sprint.

During this jam-packed semester, losing an entire Saturday was devastating. The weekend was where I could usually catch up on assignments, outline lecture notes, and squeeze a couple hours in on one or both of the CWC or DBF projects. It was all too common for a few of us to meet up on a Sunday afternoon for testing in the wind-tunnel. Still, the football games were just as much a part of the Penn State experience as our engineering classes were—we just needed to find ways to make it all work.

The only way for us to balance all this with our studies and extracurricular activities was to have a total separation of school and social life. It was like flipping an 'on-off' switch. I had a pretty amazing living situation during my junior and senior years at Penn State. I was in an apartment directly across the street from the aerospace building. The good part was that I could wake up, brew a coffee, and walk from my front door to the classroom door in a minute and a half. I often sat in class with an actual coffee mug; it was awesome. The bad part was that we had 6 guys living in a one floor apartment with one bathroom. We became pretty comfortable with each other to say the least.

The guys got used to only seeing me between the hours of 10 PM and 2 AM. My schedule involved waking up daily around six and heading to campus where I worked until around 10 PM. Those sixteen hours were filled with a mix of classes, studying, and working on the wind turbine and airplane. Most nights, I'd come home feeling completely exhausted. During the first half of the week, I'd usually just walk in, brush my teeth, and go straight to bed. A quick 5 or 6 hours would recharge me enough to repeat the cycle again the next day.

Most of my roommates were also studious engineering students, and we usually went to sleep early during the week. At least until Thursday night, and sometimes even Friday, which was a big improvement from the Tuesdays and Wednesdays I'd been doing just a year and a half earlier. It was clear that the stakes were much higher this semester and I was locked in on school. Even on the weekends, unless there was a tailgate, we were either in the aerospace building or some other quiet study spot on campus. There wasn't a minute to waste while the sun was up.

Even so, I was struggling to keep all the balls in the air that I was trying to juggle. And this was apparent—at least to myself. On the CWC team, I found it hard to track progress on the various different tasks the team was working on. We really were trying to do too much, and would have been much better off focusing on one thing and doing it extremely well. For the airplane, we just weren't making fast enough progress building the first prototype.

For some reason, I decided it was a good idea to sign up for even more. I really had a difficult time saying no to things back then, and even now I only say no with a 65% success rate. Back then I was much less successful at saying no. Unique opportunities and experiences are difficult for me to pass on, especially those that would be good for my self-development.

I'll never forget one weekend in particular when I was signed up for an early Saturday morning leadership training. I was sluggish from being out late the night before, and took my morning coffee across the street to the aerospace building. I still needed to print out some preparatory material. I was so underwater that I didn't even know what we were going to be doing at the training. The computer lab on the top floor of the aerospace building, which was one of my go-to work spots, was quiet at 8 AM on a Saturday.

There was no one else there, which wasn't entirely shocking. The majority of Penn Staters tend to have a bit of a slow start on the weekends. My eyes were still a bit crusty and my contacts hadn't quite settled down yet. I was blinking rapidly to try and straighten out my vision as I chugged some coffee in an attempt to kick-start my brain. I skimmed my emails looking for the training information when my eyes lurched to a stop on something they didn't expect to see.

The subject line said 'Rotorcraft Aeromechanics,' and the email wasn't from a name I recognized. I almost moved it to spam. But then I realized it was an '@nasa.gov' email address. The email was straightforward. "Dear Jason, We'd like for you to come to NASA Ames this spring semester for an internship." That was it. I was stunned, and initially thought it was a twisted joke—one I didn't have time or energy to deal with.

I logged out of the computer and headed to the leadership training. We were given mock scenarios that we may face someday once out in the workforce. It was run by a group of behavioral psychologists and they watched our every move as we reacted to the fictitious situations they put us in. Sometimes the psychologists were even in the scenario themselves and would purposefully act-out in an attempt to elicit an emotional response from us.

I tried to stay focused throughout the several hour long training, but my mind was wandering. 'What was that email that I'd received earlier in the morning?' I wondered to myself, or maybe even aloud. The training concluded and we'd receive our results in a few weeks. I found the psychologists to be a bit odd; they had great poker faces, not letting on to how well, or poorly, you performed. Regardless, my mind quickly shifted back to the morning's email.

I took a brisk walk to the closest computer room I could think of and logged back into my email. Despite it still being Saturday morning, a new email was sitting there. And again, it was from NASA.

"Dear Mr. Cornelius, Here is a more formal introduction. My name is Bill and I work in the Rotorcraft Aeromechanics Office at NASA Ames Research Center in Moffett Field, California. We conduct rotary wing research on all types of helicopters and other rotary wing vehicles. If you are still available and interested, we would be honored for you to join us for the spring semester."

Holy smokes! I'd done it.

I responded to Bill with a very long, cheesy email, which could have been boiled down to, "Yes Sir. Thank you, Sir. I'll be there." Texas had rubbed off on me a bit by this point.

There were a lot of unanswered questions around how to take a spring internship. When I applied at Bell over the summer, I knew my chances would be higher to get in during the spring as compared to the summer since not many students would be willing to accept a slip in their graduation date. I didn't know what it would mean for my academic studies and graduation timeline, or how I would pay rent both in State College and in California. In fact, I didn't know much of anything about how this was going to work. At that moment, however, none of this seemed to matter. I had become like my more mentally strong junior-high track coach Fred, someone who could see past the obstacles and believe that things would work out if you just put your mind to it.

I told my roommates first. None of us could really believe it and we celebrated like there was no tomorrow just in case they emailed me back saying the email was sent by mistake. I also called home the next day and told my family—they were ecstatic. In a strange turn of events, I played devil's advocate with myself to make sure going was the right decision. After all, there were going to be some pretty serious ramifications of taking the opportunity such as delaying graduation, losing money on my year-long lease, and abandoning the competition teams. But everyone I talked to said the same thing, "You have to take it."

The hardest part of it all would be breaking the news to the competition teams I was leading. I spoke with the head of the wind turbine team first. Her response was a bit less pleasant than I anticipated. "How can you do this to me?" she asked. She was clearly troubled about how the team would manage without the person leading the rotor system design. But she also recognized it was an amazing opportunity for me. Ultimately, she didn't hold it against me. I was relieved since I had been working closely with her for a few years already by this point. I made it clear that I would still be available by email and on the phone as needed. I was confident the team was in a good spot to succeed even in my absence.

Next up was the airplane competition team. I told the teaching assistant for the sailplane class the news just 15 or so minutes before class was to start, and he seemed to be in disbelief. It seemed like a bit of an over-reaction, but I suppose that was out of my control. What I didn't know was that Sal, who was the other team lead, was also leaving for the spring to pursue his own internship opportunity and had already told them about it. So both of the team leads had essentially quit within a day or two of each other, leaving the rest of the team, which was composed of freshman and sophomores, hanging out to dry.

One of the professors that guided the competition team came into our class and launched into a 15 minute tirade in front of all my peers about responsibility and following through on one's commitments. It was obvious he was talking about me and Sal, but Sal wasn't in class that day. So it was all aimed squarely at me. He really took it too far in my opinion. I sat there for a while and accepted the punishment as I felt pretty bad for abandoning the team midway through the school year. Eventually though, I asked him, "What do you want me to do, give up an internship at NASA?" For anyone else in the class that was confused up to that point—the situation became crystal clear.

The class was stunned. I don't think any of us had ever seen something so inappropriate take place in a college classroom, let alone in the aerospace engineering department. It wasn't entirely uncalled for, but it showed a lot about someone's leadership style. Looking back on it now, a civilized discussion one on one would have been the more appropriate way to handle it. 'Praise in public and criticize in private,' is a leadership phrase that comes to mind now as I look back on it. The situation really sucked; this professor's class was one of my favorites, and he taught me much of what I knew early on in my aerospace journey.

I told Sal about it later—he was furious. Had he been in class that day, he would have given it right back to the professor. Sal was a much more skilled debater than I was and didn't let people get away with that sort of thing. I'm sure he would have said enough for the both of us. The situation played out how it did though, and we would have to deal with the repercussions of our choices. No matter what was to come, we had both already committed to pursuing the fork in the road down the more unknown path.

The rest of the semester finished quickly. Sal and I were both pulled from the airplane project and not permitted to finish out the semester working with the team. This was disappointing, but it allowed me to focus my energy on the wind turbine team so they'd be able to continue on after I left.

Before the end of the semester, we tested the fully integrated system. It had a new turbine rotor, a new motor, and a new electronic automated blade control system. The turbine worked flawlessly, starting up at an extremely low wind-speed and maintaining high performance across the entire wind speed range we would test at. The team leads and faculty advisors knew how it looked compared to past years' competition. **We were going to dominate.**

I wrapped up the semester with an impressive GPA. It was supposed to be the hardest semester of my life, and it most certainly delivered on its promise. There were a few times I felt like I was walking on a high-wire as I tried to balance all the responsibilities I had signed up for. In addition to finishing up my classes, I also had to figure out what to do with my apartment.

I was going to sublet my spot to another guy so I could avoid paying two rents, but my roommates got together and decided they didn't want some random person living with them—they wouldn't agree to a sublet. They all knew my financial position and that it would be extremely hard for me to pay both rents. Two of them talked to their parents and agreed to pitch in a few extra bucks each month while I was gone to alleviate some of the burden. Two more said they didn't have any extra money to give, which although it sucked, I signed a lease and they had no legal obligation to help me out of that responsibility. The last one, who was quite possibly the wealthiest out of the group, lied saying he would pitch in and then never did. It was an unpleasant ending to an otherwise great few months living together.

Still, I was on my way. Next stop, Silicon Valley.

Some of the relationships that were damaged in those few weeks surrounding my decision to intern at NASA, whether it be in the aerospace department or a subset of my roommates, never fully recovered. It taught me a lot about the behavior of people, how they react in stressful situations, and the difference between acquaintances and true friends. Sometimes it takes a real test of a relationship to understand which one you have in front of you. These were difficult life lessons for a twenty year old, or at least for me at twenty years old.

On the project side, the result was not all that bad. The Penn State Collegiate Wind Competition team would go on to win 1st place at the Department of Energy's National competition. The optimized rotor design and control mechanism we created were combined with an electronic control system made by my Freshman dorm friends, Pat and Maysoor. Combining all that with the hand-built motors made by Mitch's part of the team led us to have the most technologically advanced turbine by a long shot. There was also a business portion to the competition this year, and luckily some very energetic and entrepreneurial business students had joined the team and helped lead us to victory.

I find it extremely interesting how we sometimes cross paths again with people from our past. Pat and Maysoor, for example, were on very different academic tracks from me. Despite Penn State being a sea of some 45,000 undergraduate students, it seemed at times to be a much smaller world than the numbers suggest. Sal and I were both set to pursue our semester-long internships, which would put us on roughly the same course schedule upon our return the next fall. Almost as if by fate, because I don't think either of us could have guessed it in the beginning, our journeys continued to become more intertwined.

This fall semester taught me that **no matter how badly you think things are going, the best path forward is consistently showing up and giving it your best.** Churchill's words were a fitting summary of this challenging time. And if you're lucky, you'll find some true friends to share the ups and downs with along the way. There was still much uncertainty about how things would play out once back at PSU. But at least for now, my focus was fully on NASA.

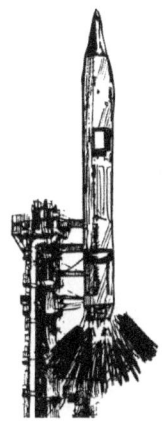

9. NASA INTERNS – ROGER BANNISTER

"Believe you can and you're halfway there."

— Theodore Roosevelt

My first NASA internship was filled with wonder and excitement. Yet throughout those four months, I often questioned whether I was truly qualified to be there—a feeling I later found was shared among many of my peers. As the youngest intern in our group and one of the youngest researchers at NASA Ames, I learned that one of the biggest factors shaping my experience was simply believing in myself and my abilities. I found that combining that belief with hard work and consistent effort meant success was not just possible—it was almost guaranteed.

My alarm went off at 3 AM on January 9, 2016. It was the classic iPhone tone that jolts you awake, but I hadn't slept a single hour anyway. I sprung out of bed and got ready for the adventure ahead. My mom and sister drove me to the Scranton International Airport, where a 6 AM flight waited to take me to Charlotte, North Carolina. I'd then catch the final leg from Charlotte to San Francisco. Flying across the country was stunning; despite having not slept, my eyes were glued to the airplane's window. It was my first time seeing the snow-capped Rocky Mountains while flying over Western United States.

They seemed to stretch on into infinity.

From San Francisco International Airport I made my way down to NASA Ames Research Center. You're greeted by several huge NASA signs as you pull onto the base at Moffett Field. Naturally, I got out and took a few pictures next to them. After clearing the first guard gate to get into the outer perimeter, the main road leads directly past a 1/6th scale wind tunnel model of the space shuttle. Even at one-sixth scale, it was larger than your typical Cessna 172 airplane.

I eventually made my way to the NASA Lodge, an old military barracks now used by the interns at Ames. The room was visibly old in both style and condition. There were two beds, a bathroom, a single desk, and a refrigerator. It was smaller than your standard hotel room, but it was home for the next four months. Rent for the Lodge was several times more than what I was used to back in Pennsylvania. And it was apparently affordable by Bay Area standards. This didn't matter to me much at the time, it was just part of what was required to be there for this once-in-a lifetime opportunity.

My roommate arrived a few hours before me and came all the way from Puerto Rico. We spent the rest of the weekend exploring the local town of Mountain View and preparing ourselves for our 1st day at NASA.

Around 9 AM on Monday, all the interns met Bill, the manager who sent me my formal invitation for the internship. Within the first three minutes, we all realized Bill was going to be an interesting supervisor. There were 10 interns in total that semester and he went one by one guessing who we were, and recounting facts about each of us from our applications. An interesting start as we each learned a bit about the rest of our intern cohort. We had three Penn Staters (myself included), my roommate from Puerto Rico, another student from Mexico, one from Texas, one from New Mexico, and three from the Royal Institute of Technology in Sweden. I was the youngest in the entire group, with several graduate students and even a PhD student or two among us.

That first day I also met my mentor for the summer, Anastasia, who was quickly becoming one of NASA's leading rotorcraft acousticians (an engineer working to make helicopters quieter). My project would involve developing code to analyze microphone signals from a prior NASA wind tunnel test of drones in the Army's 7- by 10-ft. Wind Tunnel located there at Ames. Although NASA Ames has some of the largest wind tunnels in the world, the 7- by 10-ft. is considered one of the smaller ones. You can easily walk around inside it, so it was already on a different scale than what I was used to back at Penn State. The research campus had facilities owned and operated by not only NASA, but also the Army and the Air Force.

This was all great except for one problem—I really wasn't that good at coding. The work portion of my sixteen week internship mostly consisted of Anastasia turning me into a coding pro as I took the microphone signals and turned them into meaningful data so we could quantify the 'loudness' of one drone versus another.

During the first few weeks I also had the opportunity to help the Army engineers with an active wind tunnel test in the 7- by 10. It was hard to believe that in my first first week on the job I was helping run a test in one of the nations premier aerospace testing facilities. The wind tunnel was operated at reduced pressure, which required you to go through an airlock to access the control room. It was like something straight out of a submarine movie.

Once inside, the control room had several stations, each with their own dials, switches, and monitors to control the tunnel and the model being tested. As a rotorcraft test facility, massive blast shields sat between the test section and the control room to protect the test team in the event of a catastrophic failure. The employees were all amazing; they taught me about wind tunnel testing, model preparation, and so much more. I spent hours a day asking the tunnel operator questions about the facility and past test programs that came through.

The first week was a whirl-wind. I was getting into work daily by about 6 AM and staying until at least 6 PM every day. I knew the other students were well ahead of me in experience and skill, but what I lacked in skill I would make up for in time and effort. Throughout the entire semester I continued to work at least 50-60 hours per week. This was definitely not encouraged but I had one shot to prove I was worth keeping around. Anastasia was a really amazing mentor as well. Not only was she a brilliant coder, but she was also motivating and didn't even seem to notice that I was the youngest one there. Belief, backed by hard and consistent work.

Each Friday of the internship we'd meet Bill in the conference room for a 'Taste of California History' (TOCH). He'd tell us some random facts about the state, often linked to events that would be happening in the following few days. On this first TOCH, Bill told us about the Spanish Missions in California that were linked to Spain's efforts to colonize the Western portion of America in the early 1800s. I learned that California didn't become part of the United States until 1850, by which point my ancestors were already in Pennsylvania.

After our history lesson, Bill read us an email he received from Dr. Jeanette Epps, US Astronaut and former Aeromechanics Office intern under Bill. She was doing Russian language immersion training just outside of Moscow at the Yuri Gagarin Cosmonaut Training Center, which is the main Russian cosmonaut training location. Jeanette signed her email partially in Russian, "From freezing cold Москва" (from freezing cold Moscow). It wouldn't be too long before I personally knew what she was referring to.

I thought her email was the coolest thing ever. Bill had a thematic way of presenting things. He proceeded to tell us there was a rocket launch at Vandenberg Air Force Base (now Vandenberg Space Force Base) that weekend, and that our group of interns should make the drive down to see the launch and explore the Spanish Missions. It was time for a road trip.

We loaded into the cars early on a Friday morning. A red Nissan Altima and a blue Subaru Outback were enough for the entire group. Vandenberg is a few hours south of NASA Ames and we decided to take the scenic Coastal Highway 1 for our first road trip. We were easily distracted by the amazing sights all the way down, pulling off the road for a 'quick' pit stop every 30-40 minutes. The drive ended up taking much longer than it should have, but we were all new in California and were enjoying the journey.

Eventually we made it to Vandenberg, specifically to a location where our Google search had told us was a good place to watch the launch from. We arrived at a strange scene—a SpaceX watch party. They had their own VIP tent for employees to mingle in as they waited for the launch. Us plebeians stood outside in the chilly January mist as we waited for the launch. The group just met a few days prior but we were meshing extraordinarily well. We were already cracking inside jokes and learning more about each other as we waited.

The SpaceX tent had a countdown timer inside, I guess they were watching the live feed of the televised launch. When the timer hit zero, everyone looked in the general direction we thought the rocket should be. It was so misty, verging on foggy, that we couldn't see anything. Visibility was less than the distance we were to the rocket. Still, a few seconds later we were struck with the awesome roar of the Falcon 9 Merlin engines. We still couldn't see anything, but the roar of the rocket blasting off to space is something everyone should experience at least once in their life. The group found it rather comical that we couldn't actually see the rocket. But to us, we were just happy to be there.

The trip continued on; we stayed a night in an old log cabin in Santa Ynez, made a pit stop in Santa Barbara, and then explored several Spanish Missions on the way home. I emailed Bill during the trip about the whole experience, and to thank him again for inviting me to NASA. I also told him I'd been thinking about Jeanette a good bit more since our first TOCH. It was the first time I realized that someone with a rotorcraft engineering background could help advance human discovery in space. I didn't know exactly what that meant for me, but I knew I wanted to be part of something much bigger than myself.

Looking back on it now, it reminds me of the story of Roger Bannister—the first person to run a mile in under four minutes. The world considered it impossible and doctors claimed one's heart would literally explode. The barrier stood firm for many years. But as soon as Roger ran the first sub-four minute mile, many people immediately began breaking the barrier. Sometimes just seeing another person do something is all you need to see it as a possibility for yourself. Jeanette's story was a bit like that. I saw a successful role model in NASA that mixed aerospace engineering, Russian, and even SCUBA diving, to support NASA's mission of exploring our universe.

I told Bill later that week I would learn Russian and become involved in NASA's human spaceflight program someday. It must have been either the excitement of our Vandenberg trip or the sleep deprivation that possessed me to say such an outlandish thing. Frankly, I had no idea what I was talking about or what I was getting myself into. For some reason, it just seemed like the natural thing to do. Bill was completely supportive; he saw something for me that I couldn't yet see for myself. I learned the value that week of **believing in someone else's belief in you until your belief kicks in.**

The weeks at Ames started flying off the calendar as we packed them to the brim with work, social activities, and exploring all California has to offer. It seemed like every weekend we were on the move to see something new. Aside from our individual projects, there were also events and seminars that we'd often go to. One such event was called, "Interstellar Flight and Search for Extraterrestrial Intelligence." It was a one hour discussion where NASA engineers and scientists discussed the idea of traveling at the speed of light to reach Alpha Centauri—the closest star to our own sun.

It was shocking. We were seated in this large lecture hall on the NASA campus and the speaker was visiting from another research institution abroad. I think my jaw must have been on the floor as they fervently discussed the very real future of reaching another star, collecting data, and sending it back to Earth. The lecture and the follow-on discussion confirmed the fact that we were in one of the coolest places in the entire world for an aerospace engineering student.

On the weekends that we hadn't planned a trip, I could be found in a coffee shop on Castro Street in Mountain View. Le Boulanger is a bakery and coffee shop with multiple locations mostly in Northern California. They had free wifi and free unlimited coffee refills, so I staked out a space in the back corner for a few hours on several Saturday and Sunday mornings. They softly played calm background music—the kind you could bop to slightly while you were in the zone working. A low buzz filled the cafe as folks came in for breakfast and later lunch.

I focused on two main activities in that coffee shop. The first was Russian; I wanted to get a head start before launching into Introductory Russian back at Penn State. The language was tough—even learning the alphabet took many hours of practice. I found some online resources to start my studies for free. At the time I had no idea what I was doing, but I felt like I was at least doing something.

My second major focus was writing scholarship applications. I had been applying non-stop to any and all scholarships I was eligible for both internal at Penn State and external across the nation. In the beginning, some combination of my resume not being that special and my writing being deplorable resulted in me getting almost no traction. In my first two years, I applied to at least one or two dozen and secured only 3. The financial aid from these awards was monumentally beneficial, but I was still taking out massive loans.

As it turned out, the way to get better at writing was to write. But this obvious conclusion was not the one I wanted to hear. I hated writing, and considered it a massive waste of time. "Why does one need to write," I wondered. "What's wrong with a life of math and physics?" I had clearly led myself very far astray at one point or another. Luckily, my desire to reduce the financial burden on my family for me pursuing my dream outweighed my disdain for writing. As a reminder, when I took the SAT's in high school, I scored around the 50th percentile in reading and writing despite scoring 99th percentile in the nation for math. I clearly had some remedial work to do. And remedial work we did. The more I wrote, the better I got.

That spring I applied to numerous scholarships, and much to my surprise, I started receiving them. I secured the second highest award of my Fraternity's national scholarship competition along with various awards from several organizations I was involved in. All of these together would pay for a considerable chunk of my senior year at Penn State, and enabled me to focus on my studies.

It felt like I was firing on all cylinders. It was probably the most productive period of my entire life. I was making great progress with my microphone noise project, and was building a reputation as a hard worker within the group. Some of the older interns preached work-life balance to me, but I didn't have time to think much about it back then. The week was reserved for focused and diligent work.

A few special occasions did pull me away from the office, though. One such event was Air Force One landing on the Moffett Field runway. Air Force One is the airplane that carries the President, and it lands right next to my office any time the president visits northern California. I stood outside all day waiting for that plane. We knew the plane was landing at some point, just not exactly what time. Late in the afternoon, I saw President Barack Obama step out of the Boeing 747 onto the staircase he would traverse down to the tarmac. It was the first time I'd seen a US president in person (though I was still quite a distance away thanks to the very serious security).

We also got to watch the Navy's Blue Angel squadron practicing for their flyover of Super Bowl 50. They practiced at Moffett for the same reason the president landed there—it's a secure federal airfield. We got used to the roar of their engines as they practiced their routine all week. We'd often spend hours sitting outside watching them rip around the South Bay as they tracked their route to Levi Stadium.

On the day of the superbowl, all six airplanes took the runway together in a diamond formation. One lead F/A-18 Hornet, two in the next row, and three in the last row. We were inside the NASA perimeter next to our building, which was adjacent to the far end of the runway. The roar of the jet engines during takeoff reverberated off the surrounding buildings and reached us long before we saw any sign of the planes coming our way. Next thing we knew, all six aircraft zipped past us nearly at eye level, they must have been moving at two-to-three hundred miles per hour. Then out of nowhere, they ripped skyward. It was the fourth or fifth time I revised my opinion of 'the coolest thing I'd ever seen' that spring.

Even at work, there were many things to do besides our projects and attending seminars. I made a point of reaching out to NASA employees throughout my time there. I could always think of useful questions to ask them about their career choices, their time at NASA, and their current position. It was an amazing opportunity to learn what possibilities could be waiting for me some day. In late April, I spoke with the NASA Ames Chief Scientist and NASA Johnson's Assistant Director for the Commercial Crew Program. I found the full-time employees, no matter how busy they might have been, always energized when talking with interns. Those discussions helped immensely as I looked to the future.

As we neared the end of our time at NASA, we had one final trip to take—a road-trip to Los Angeles. We had several major stops on the itinerary, and we started with another visit to Vandenberg Air Force Base. We witnessed another SpaceX launch carrying supplies to the International Space Station. It was a day-time launch, and we just parked along the road this time to watch with many other spectators. The rocket ripped through the sky in a blaze of glory. Although it was again cloudy near the coast, we at least caught a quick glimpse of the rocket on its skyward journey. It was the first time SpaceX successfully landed the first stage on a drone ship at sea, which many up to that point considered impossible. Our perception of what was possible was constantly challenged throughout the internship in the most amazing ways.

After the launch, we continued down the coast to Venice Beach where we stayed for one night to explore the scene in LA. Several of our European interns had stayed in hostels back home, so we decided to give Venice Beach hostels a try. Each of us was allotted a hard boiled egg and one slice of toast in the morning for breakfast. The worker seemed like he'd witnessed some crazy things in the area—it was an experience to say the least. We explored Muscle Beach, the Santa Monica Pier, and even made a stop by Disney's Universal Studios. One of our Swedish interns was an avid Harry Potter fan and wore a Hogwarts robe all day in the park. While in LA, we couldn't miss the opportunity to see the names of Neil Armstrong, Buzz Aldrin, and Michael Collins on the Hollywood Walk of Fame for their trip to the moon aboard Apollo 11 in 1969. Having seen that, our LA expedition was complete and we headed home to close out the internship.

My four months at NASA taught me more than I could have imagined. I worked long hours to take full advantage of what I considered to be the opportunity of a lifetime. Being the youngest in our group of interns had a lot of growing pains associated with it, but I transformed throughout the semester as I observed my more senior peers.

I felt proud of the work I accomplished throughout my time there, including a hefty final report documenting all the code I developed for the microphone signal processing. We spent one last night or two together on the main street in Mountain View as we looked back on our shared experience together from the past few months. By this point I knew the drill. It was likely I wouldn't see most of them again for a few years. And quite possibly some of them never again in my life as we fanned out across the world.

For me, I was due in Beijing International Airport in about a week's time for another one month trip across China. Penn State was sending me this time around as the course's teaching assistant. After the one month trip, I'd have 36 hours before catching another flight to Texas for my second Bell internship I committed to at the end of the previous summer. It felt like I was blasting off on my own Falcon 9 rocket. The coming months promised to be a whirlwind of excitement.

I drew a few major takeaways from my first internship at NASA. One of them was the power of being articulate. As I observed those around me who were good with words, I realized the immense power held within them. My consistent effort on the weekends to fill out scholarship applications significantly improved my writing ability. Despite how useless a pursuit I initially considered it to be, becoming articulate in my speech and writing has been one of the largest determining factors in my success.

One of the most critical life lessons I took away was that it's okay to get started by believing in someone else's belief in you. Another person's faith can serve as a powerful call to action, helping you see potential you might not yet see in yourself. But eventually, we must all become our own biggest believers. In my first week at Ames, Bill saw something in me I hadn't yet discovered in myself. He gave me two invaluable things—an inspiring goal to aim at and his total belief that I'd achieve it. Over the course of the internship, I began to see that vision too, building the confidence needed to follow through and pursue it on my own.

CHALLENGE 6

Roger Bannister

Think about your goal or the future you're working toward. Is there someone who has already achieved it or done something similar? How can you learn from their path?

Write down the name of one person you admire in this space. If you don't know anyone personally, find an inspiring figure in a book, podcast, or online video. Research a specific action they took to succeed, and think about how you could replicate or adapt it to your journey.

Remember, "Birds of a feather flock together." Surround yourself—virtually or in real life—with people who inspire you, and watch how it transforms your mindset.

10. CHINA AND TEXAS TAKE 2 – MR. MOTIVATOR

"Twenty years from now you will be more disappointed by the things that you didn't do than by the ones you did do. So throw off the bowlines. Sail away from the safe harbor. Catch the trade winds in your sails. Explore. Dream. Discover."

— Mark Twain

Throughout my journey, I was often faced with the choice to stick with the familiar or venture into the unknown. These opportunities usually came in unexpected ways. When a unique experience presents itself, we must decide between the comfort of what we know and the growth found in forging into the unknown. For me, I've always leaned toward the latter. My escapades over the years have taken me far from home, led to long stretches without seeing friends and family, and even delayed my journey from point A to point B. Looking back, every experience was worth it—they taught me new ways to see the world. *"Two roads diverged in a wood, and I—I took the one less traveled by, And that has made all the difference."*— Robert Frost

1. Back to China

I landed at Beijing International Airport on May 5th, 2016, less than a week after finishing my internship at NASA. The airport is one of the busiest in the world and seemed even more lively than my first time there two years prior. I came to China for the same program I went on after freshman year, but this time Penn State's College of Engineering sent me to assist Dr. Wu as a teaching assistant. My role came with responsibilities such as acting as a mentor and leader for the students, speaking on behalf of our group on formal occasions, and generally keeping an eye on everyone.

We dove into the trip with a similar itinerary to my first time in China. It was fascinating to revisit several places I had seen two years earlier and discover new things about them that I didn't catch the first time. Only having a few hours in each location meant that we really had to make the most of our time. We'd often interact with the locals around us while waiting for Professor Wu to get us squared away for the various activities we had on the agenda. Again, several native Chinese Penn State students came on the trip to help us interact with our environment. They helped us immensely in breaking the language barrier between our English speaking group and the Chinese locals. Still, many of them would see more of their country on this trip than they, or other Chinese people, have ever seen in their lives.

Qifeng ("Chee-fung") was one of the Chinese students on the trip this year and introduced himself as Steve to other Americans. Steve moved to the US for high school and then joined Penn State's mechanical engineering department. This led him to be the most 'Americanized' Chinese student on the trip, with a deep understanding of American culture and a commanding grasp of the language. All these attributes made him sort of like the lead Chinese assistant on the trip that could help us navigate any situation we ran into. We would work together quite a bit throughout the trip to help Dr. Wu.

The first week was mostly a blur, just as I remembered from my first time around. The schedule in Beijing was demanding, and even free minutes between activities were filled with learning about the backgrounds of our 44-student group. The group was definitely ready to slightly reduce the pace after our escapades in China's capital.

We arrived at my favorite city in China, Dalian. One of our first activities was stopping by a local grade school; it seemed the entire student body prepared weeks for our visit. There was a huge banner hanging over the front of the school welcoming their friends from Penn State. One group sang traditional Chinese songs to us; the talent of these children was seriously amazing. Another group performed a choreographed dance with traditional Chinese touches. The final stop was an entire play! The air was filled with a positive sense of joy.

Despite the language barrier, it was easy for us to see how much the visit meant to the students. We found that in most cases we didn't even need translation to communicate; it was as if we were communicating on some lower childhood-like plane that didn't need spoken words to make sense. At one point our hosts led us outside. We weren't too certain what was going on, but next thing we knew the courtyard adjacent to the school was rapidly filling with what seemed to be hundreds on the verge of thousands of students. They were all wearing the same school uniform; clearly a strict dress code was in effect. And they made extremely precise and tight rows. The Chinese national anthem came on the loudspeaker and the army of students sang in unison. On one hand it was familiar—singing the national anthem during the school day as I did growing up in Pennsylvania. On the other hand, something about it seemed very different. From the uniforms to the tight rows, it was a glimpse into China that I don't think many outsiders would ever see.

Xinli's friends in Dalian hosted us again for exquisite dinners. Our group was so big that we couldn't all be seated around the gargantuan automated table we dined at before. A majority of the group sat there and ate together, with a small side room for overflow. In an interesting turn of events, Xinli, our host, me, Steve, and a few others (about 10 of us in total) sat in the overflow room. I guess this made it more like the VIP room with Xinli and the host.

This was the CEO of the cigarette manufacturing plant and the room filled with smoke as we sampled the seafood delicacies before us. It was an interesting scene—everyone in the room took turns making speeches with Steve as our lead translator. Toasts were an important part of Chinese culture, or at least the part of it we were being exposed to. All the students would have several opportunities to practice their public speaking in front of a large audience of their peers and VIPs. It was actually some great practical training.

We continued on our journey leaving Dalian via an overnight sleeper train. Each of the train cars had several cabins inside and a single bathroom.

The cabins were laid out with a set of bunk beds off to the left and another to the right. Between the beds was a small plastic table just large enough to put a few glasses on.

The train was delayed a few hours so we boarded late in the evening, and it would take us the whole night to get to our destination near the Yangtze river. Our group became pretty tight knit by this point in the trip, though of course some smaller sub-groups formed within the larger class. I hung out with Professor Wu and some of the others, many of us crammed into a single cabin, as we played card games and cracked jokes late into the night. Luckily our group filled the entire wagon, otherwise I think we would have been reprimanded over noise complaints throughout the night.

One of the cars was a restaurant that we eventually made our way to. It was a good break from the cramped conditions in the cabins and we were able to interact with some of the other Chinese travelers on the train.

There's something about being there together, traveling in the same direction on an overnight train, that seemed to transcend both cultural and language barriers. We were somewhere in-between sign language and a game of charades, but our communication with the other Chinese travelers was effortless and fun.

I would find many times throughout this trip and others that spoken language is needed to convey facts, instructions, and details, but not to express many of the human emotions. A simple smile, a shake of the hand, a hug—these actions communicated their meaning perfectly. This made me realize that every day we have entire dialogues with people without uttering a single word. This realization has made me think very carefully about how I interact with people today. Even without saying a word, you've already told others how you are feeling just by how you carry yourself. So be mindful of what message you want to send out.

We eventually made it to Shanghai where Steve knew the area quite well. He took a handful of us on the first day there to a famous local restaurant for Shanghai juicy dumplings (小笼包 xiǎo lóng bāo). Juicy dumplings are one of my favorite foods in the entire world, along with hot pot of course. The restaurant was a hole in the wall type of place, but it was jam packed so we knew we were in for a treat. We demolished platter after platter of the juicy dumplings using the special etiquette Steve showed us for how to eat them. You need to first place one on your spoon using your chopsticks, then take a small bite out of the side, suck out the juice, and then you can finally eat the dumpling. It was an art form. The locals seemed impressed by the sheer quantity we ate.

We also stopped by ExxonMobil this time around and were able to meet with several American expats and Chinese citizens working there in the labs. I wondered what it would be like to live and work abroad for an extended period of time. Even on this trip, being on the other side of the world for just a few weeks seemed like a lot. I didn't know if my work would lead me abroad someday, but I was now open to the idea of it from my travels through China. I found that being in completely unfamiliar situations were the times I grew the most, and often had the most fun as well.

My last and arguably most important task in Shanghai was to find Bun Man (the guy that sold me and Paul the spicy pork-filled buns two years prior). I traced my steps as best as I could remember from two years earlier. We were staying in a different part of the city, but luckily he was close to the Bund area giving me some great reference points. After some slight searching, I found him in the exact spot I left him two years before. This gave me a lot of food for thought quite literally as I ate many of his delicious pork buns. "What would it be like to do the same thing every day in the same place for two years straight?" I asked some of the other students that were with me. How many years had he been showing up there on this busy Shanghai street to make and sell his pork buns. It seemed like a hard job—what was it that kept him showing up there every day? These were all good questions for me to ponder on the 14-hour flight home.

I made it through another intense month traveling China, with a plethora of interesting and exciting tales to tell for years to come. But there was no time to think about it all. I had less than 36 hours to swap my belongings at home from backpacking China to professional attire before heading down to Bell. I remember the pace of these adventures with quick turn-arounds between each being quite exciting. I'm sure it was frustrating for some of my family, but I was on a mission to pack as much into each day, week, and month as I could manage.

My short one-month trip in China taught me more about human interactions, and gave me a still better appreciation for people with different backgrounds and perspectives. I developed the ability to hear opposing views of the world and rationally analyze them. Bun man, for example, was a product of his circumstances just as I was a product of mine. He stood on the street every day because that is what he knew. I couldn't fathom the monotony of such a life. But then again, I didn't need to. That was his life—not mine.

This is likely the best skill I developed in all my travels, and one that I feel is severely lacking in America today. The ability to be okay with how others choose to live their life, even if it's very different from how I choose to live mine. It would still take more time to internalize this final thought, but I was beginning to understand that each and every single one of us thinks differently. And that's what makes this world an interesting place.

2. Mr. Motivator

Connor, my roommate from my first Bell internship, picked me up from the Dallas airport around 11 AM. Dallas Fort Worth gets hot in the summer, but it's a very dry heat. Connor often reminded me, "This ain't nothing compared to Houston boy." At least this time around I was used to his Texas accent. Regardless, the temperatures in DFW can soar well above 100 degrees—and they sure did.

We still had Connor's 66' Mustang, which was really good since both of us were working at Bell's flight test facility called XworX this summer. XworX was around 20 to 30 minutes from the Bell headquarters where we worked the summer prior. Our apartment was somewhere in the middle of the two locations and we shared it with two other interns: one in Finance and another in engineering.

We'd take Connor's car at the crack of dawn to beat the Texas sun. Neither of us were really morning people, but luckily during my NASA journey I found some good YouTube videos that pump you up for work. Initially I listened to upbeat electronic dance music (EDM), but every so often I'd put on a specific motivational video that I listened to since high school. It was a mix of the Rocky soundtrack overlaid with some other clips from various inspirational movie scenes. I'd play this and sit at my desk in quiet contemplation whenever I needed a reminder of why I was working so hard.

Eventually, the YouTube algorithm started suggesting similar motivational and inspirational content to me. I stumbled upon motivational speakers such as Zig Ziglar, Les Brown, Tony Robbins, and Jim Rohn. Each speaker had their own style and type of message, but they were all generally empowering and uplifting figures that seemed larger than life. Les's story resonated with my own—he spoke passionately about the many hardships he encountered on his journey towards his dream. Les's largest motivating force was that he had to succeed so he could take care of his mother.

Connor was always up for new experiences; so in the summer of 2016 we ripped down the Texas freeway at 6 AM, with the windows down since there was no AC, and Les Brown speaking affirmations into our still sleeping minds. "You don't have to be great to get started, but you have to get started to be great." "Other people's opinion of you does not have to become your reality." "You must be willing to do the things today others won't do in order to have the things tomorrow others won't have." "When life knocks you down, try to land on your back. Because if you can look up, you can get up!" We strained to hear him, maybe because the windows were down on the highway, or because we were still sleeping, but his main and most persistent message was clear:

"It's. Not. Over. Until. You. Win."

Connor and I were on a spiritual journey together as we expanded our thinking that summer on the Texas commute. During the first week of the internship, we had an orientation put on by human resources. There were around 130 interns across the entire company participating in the orientation. I knew the HR department from the summer prior, and they asked me if I wanted to say a few words to our intern cohort.

By this point, I'd become reasonably confident in my public speaking skills and enjoyed the challenge of trying to connect with an audience. I prepared a 5 minute speech, got up, and gave it. I can barely remember anything from the moment I started speaking until the time I stopped. But when I uttered my final words, a roar erupted from the room. I don't know what I did that was so successful, but whatever it was, it landed. Some of the other interns would call me 'Mr. Motivator' for the rest of the summer. Hearing Les and the others had paid off.

At XWorkx, Connor and I were both supporting the Bell 525 Relentless helicopter flight test program. We sat in some makeshift office space attached to the hanger with the first three helicopters produced for flight testing. It was probably the coolest setup an engineering intern could ask for; we had our desks and computers to work on, but at any time could make the 30 second walk into the hangar to get up close to the hardware.

Connor was working in a manufacturing group that would work through how the 525 would eventually be mass-produced. He was a nuts and bolts type of guy, often working on his Mustang on the weekends. I was just a few cubicles over in the Flight Technology Research and Development group. The group had many advanced degree holders and tackled some of the toughest problems faced by the company.

My project involved engine inlet icing, which could cause major problems for the aircraft. I simulated the engine icing conditions using computer models similar to my previous Bell internship, but instead of analyzing the structural strength I was analyzing the airflow around the helicopter. We needed to understand what flying into icing conditions meant for the vehicle's performance and safety.

The coolest part about being at XWorX had to be the actual flight testing. Pilots flew the new aircraft to expand our understanding of its operational capability. The flight test team had a daily morning brief between the pilots, test director, and engineers where we reviewed the day's flight plan. The atmosphere in the room was generally light-hearted, and the pilots were just as cool as you would imagine. Most were retired military flight test pilots with thousands of hours of flight experience under their belts.

Flight testing was a lot of fun. Everyone was high-energy and fast-paced as we worked to improve the capabilities of the aircraft. In those early days I didn't have much appreciation yet for the risk involved in expanding the envelope of new aerospace vehicles. It all seemed like a normal day at the office, until one day it wasn't.

[Technical details and facts from the following section are public record from the National Transportation Safety Board (NTSB)].

Wednesday July 6th started out like any other day at XWorkx. I sat in our morning flight test brief, then made my way up to the control room where the engineers monitored the aircraft's data stream and communicated with the pilots to work through the test plan. The room was medium sized, with just three or four rows of desks and a few computer stations in each row. The stations were for monitoring all the data coming back from the aircraft in real time. I sat in the middle row with a headset on watching the pilots work.

Over the headset I could hear the dialogue between the test director and the pilots. The whole team was listening in as we moved from point to point in the run card. We were doing high-speed one-engine-inoperative testing. This means we simulated losing one of the aircraft's two engines to ensure the pilots could fly the aircraft to safety. The pilots successfully performed the test at increasingly faster speeds approaching the aircraft's velocity never exceed (VNE) speed. VNE is an aerospace term used to identify the maximum rated limit for an aircraft's safe flight speed.

A few seconds into one of the test points, it was clear something out of the ordinary was happening. Then suddenly the telemetry screens froze and the video feed went blank. The room fell silent as the test director repeatedly called to the pilots for a reply—one that would never come.

We made our way back to our desks to await further news. All we knew so far was that the aircraft likely crash landed about 50 miles away from XWorx. There was an eerie feeling throughout the office but it seemed folks were maintaining hope. Though I don't think anyone accomplished any work for the rest of the day. An hour or two later, the XWorkx team gathered in the large conference room for an update. There wasn't really any way to sugarcoat it—both pilots died in the crash landing. It was difficult news for a 21 year old to process.

Connor and I left work early that day. He hadn't been in the control room so I filled him in on the drive home. Back then, I was still very young and didn't fully understand the full complexity of helicopters, or aerospace vehicles in general for that matter. The team would eventually re-create the events leading to the incident, which was later published by the NTSB. "The probable cause of the accident was a severe vibration of the helicopter that led to the crew's inability to maintain sufficient rotor rotation speed."

The atmosphere in the office for weeks to come would be rather bleak. Some engineers, especially those in the control room, felt some responsibility for what had happened. Some of them retracted into their work, others were visibly stressed, and a select few seemed normal (on the outside at least). In the span of a few seconds, XWorkx went from being the coolest place for an aerospace engineering intern to work, to being the most sobering.

The tragedy rocked the company from top to bottom as the first time in Bell's long 80-year history that it lost its own pilots in flight testing. Connor and I attended funeral services with what seemed like several hundred Bell employees. One of the test pilot's brothers spoke at the memorial service; he broke down on the stage pleading with the audience to not make the mistake he did of losing touch with his family. The entire ordeal gave me a lot to think about.

All the events surrounding the incident taught me at a very young age the seriousness of what it meant to choose a career in aerospace and the risks involved with pushing the boundaries of flight. I also received lessons in personal accountability, engineering ethics, and forgiveness. I witnessed forgiveness from the family, forgiveness from the company, and forgiveness of oneself. Each person would come to terms in their own time, in order to move forward.

Connor and I worked for a while at the headquarters building for a break from the stifling environment at XWorkx. My work involved a lot of coding, which luckily I was a pro at from working with Anastasia at NASA. The math was challenging, but I threw myself into the project. Connor and I continued our usual cycle of work, gym, and adventures around the DFW area. Despite our dedication to the gym and our diets, we sometimes found ourselves having honey butter chicken biscuits and huge milkshakes at Whataburger. Hey, we had to enjoy the fruits of our labor.

A little over mid-way through the internship, I had a call with Penn State's Aerospace Engineering department head. I wanted to found a high-power rocketry club back at PSU and needed approval from the department head to do it. I was always on the lookout for opportunities to improve my resume, and I suppose founding the club went along with my aspirations to continue on at NASA. My only qualifications, however, were that I launched a few Estes model rockets growing up and loved the movie, 'October Sky.' (A must see for anyone that has never watched it.)

The department head did some research before the call since he didn't know me all too well at that time. He spoke with a few of my aerospace professors to get their opinion on me, "They feel that despite your good intentions you sometimes sign up for more than you should. It can be better to focus on fewer things and do them well than overload yourself and do poorly." The words stung and at the moment I thought he was wrong. But who was I to argue with the head of aerospace engineering? The rocketry club wasn't going to happen.

I hadn't yet reached the age of appreciating the wisdom of my elders. It would still be a few years before I would find myself truly receptive to advice opposing the direction I wanted to go. My youthful ignorance made me feel as if I somehow knew the world better, after a short 20 years on this rock flying through space, than folks who had been here two or three times longer than me. In the end, I've decided that youthful ignorance (no matter your age) can be very beneficial to making transformative advancements. But there's certainly a balance between going with your intuition, and heeding the wisdom given to you by your elders. It would take me years to find that balance.

A few weeks later we came to the end of the internship, which is when Bell makes offers for positions. The summer prior I committed to my follow-on internship before leaving Bell, but this time would be different.

My supervisor and I sat down one day in a conference room. The room was well lit yet small. There was a table with enough space for four or five people. He was a busy guy and didn't beat around the bush. "What do you want to do with your future?" he asked. I wondered to myself internally, 'What the heck kind of question is that?' The truth is, I had no idea. I loved working at Bell, but NASA was my dream, and several more years of graduate school to get my PhD were in the mix as well. "I need to focus on school," was all I could think to say. "They'll pressure you to take a full-time job unless you want me to tell them to leave you alone," he said, "They might try to make you an offer you can't refuse."

I knew what this meant. Bell put a lot of energy into training me from a young intern during that one-week long boot camp to the engineer I had become. My time there covered a host of real world experiences and led to an amazing practical skill set. They would make me a very generous offer to lock me in after graduation.

I knew that I wanted to do grad school, however, and didn't want the temptation of a job offer to steer me off track. "I need to focus on school. I really don't want to see an offer because I don't know if I'd be able to turn it down," I told him. And that was the truth—I had made peanuts for money throughout my life up to that point, and dangling a nice private-sector engineering salary in front of me would have been very challenging to say no to. It's true that money is not everything, but it does drive the experiences we can have throughout our lives.

It was an interesting encounter. My supervisor was going to shield me from the company because he knew the value of me going straight into graduate school full-time and not getting distracted by starting to work. He gave me the choice and supported me once I made my decision; the interaction taught me a lot about what it means to be a manager versus a leader. Sometimes in life we're faced with a hard choice between what's best for someone who trusts you as a mentor and what's best for the organization. I've seen this decision play out around me on several occasions—sometimes the mentor chose me, sometimes they chose the organization. **Both experiences taught me the type of leader I wanted to be.**

Our meeting was the last I heard of returning offers that summer. I left Bell in mid-August after buttoning up my work projects. It was the last time

I'd see Connor and many of the other Bell folks for several years as I pursued my graduate education at Penn State.

One week at home is all I had time for before I was to return to Penn State for my senior year. I was getting used to the break-neck schedule, but I wondered if life would ever slow down again.

CHALLENGE 7

As Bad As You Want to Breathe

Think of a time when you considered giving up on a goal. Write down what motivated you to keep going (or what could have motivated you if you didn't). Now think about the goal you've been working with throughout these challenges and the obstacles you predict will come up along the way. What reasons will you have to keep you going when the going gets tough? Are you truly committed to seeing it through?

11. DIVERSIFYING INTERESTS

"When you want to succeed as bad as you want to breathe that's when you'll be successful."

— Unknown

Returning to Penn State after an 8-month adventure at NASA, China, and Bell felt like riding a big wave, one that would only stop if I decided to jump off. Nowadays I enjoy surfing in California and the big waves are exhilarating. But if you wipe out, you better take a deep breath, hold it, and hope for the best. This semester at Penn State was like a big wave: my adventure was still accelerating, and my only options were to sink or swim. Most of the time, I felt like I was going under, and I even learned the very literal meaning of the above quote.

The first semester of my senior year at Penn State promised to be another challenging one. Mid-to-late August in State College typically had hot weather, which was a nice entry before we progressively plunged into a frozen tundra for the next six months. I had a full course load of aerospace classes and also signed up for Introductory Russian and SCUBA diving. I was so inspired by the email from Dr. Jeanette Epps that I decided these activities would be neat to add into my life. They were totally unrelated to my aerospace studies. And to most people, I was just doing them for fun. There was a small chance they'd help me in my career someday, but only if I took a pretty major departure from my current career track.

During my time at Bell a few months earlier, I had also emailed my German aerospace professor, Dr. Sven Schmitz. My email detailed my recent experiences at NASA and Bell, and I asked Sven if I could do independent research with him. He agreed to it and research with him rounded out the rest of my schedule.

The first week of classes was intense. On top of the jubilant reunion I was having with friends, my first two Russian classes were incredible. Our teacher was actually Ukrainian, but as I'd come to learn, almost anyone over the age of 30 from a former Soviet Union country was fluent in Russian. She seemed to me about as Slavic as one got. She had a passion and excitement to teach us the beauty and complexity of the Russian language and culture. It was as if to study the language one must also study the culture. Russian class seemed like an amazing choice.

The first day of SCUBA didn't go nearly as well. I found out one week before the start of classes that we'd have to do a swim test. 'No big deal,' I thought. I'd been swimming since I was a few years old. The swim test consisted of swimming one length of the pool underwater, a 300 meter freestyle swim in under nine minutes, and ten minutes of treading water. I felt pretty good about the underwater swim and treading water—though 10 minutes did sound a bit long. Although I never truly swam laps before, I figured it was similar enough to splashing around in a pool like I'd done for longer than I could remember. I checked out a YouTube video on how to do the proper freestyle swim form and called it good.

SCUBA class was held at Penn State's natatorium building where our division one swim team practiced and competed. The indoor pools were a safe haven from the harsh State College Winter, but the water temperature of the competition pool was kept low. The varsity swimmers were working out after all, so the colder water prevented them from overheating. The room was massive on the inside, there was the full sized competition pool, a 14-ft. dive-well, and another full-length practice pool. The natatorium smelled strongly of chlorine, the sharp scent a constant reminder of the intense training that took place there.

We met Tim that morning, Penn State's Dive Safety Officer and the main instructor for PSU's dive program. He's a professor in the College of Earth and Mineral Sciences and conducts a large amount of his research underwater. It was immediately apparent that Tim was a no nonsense kind of guy—he was stern and serious. SCUBA diving, after all, was a very serious activity. Although the conditions in the natatorium were controlled with several layers of safety, SCUBA diving in the real world is one of the most dangerous hobbies behind only skydiving, rock climbing, and riding motorcycles.

Tim briefed us that morning on how the swim test would be conducted, and the nerves among the class were palpable. We had several relatively fit looking students in the group, myself included.

We started with the underwater swim. Tim went first- he jumped into the deep end of the competition pool feet first, touched the bottom, and then slowly started swimming. All eyes were glued on him as he slowly frog-kicked the length of the pool underwater without coming up for air. One by one, the new students jumped in and attempted the swim. A majority of us made it, including myself, but two or three panicked midway and surfaced, gasping for air. The underwater swim is entirely a mental test—the average person could swim down and back two times before the brain becomes starved of oxygen and blacks out. In the moment, though, even one length of the pool seemed like a gargantuan feat.

Next it was time for the 300 meter swim. We jumped in the pool and were hanging off the wall. At Tim's signal, I kicked off the wall as hard as I could and started to do a very embarrassing attempt at a freestyle swim. I immediately started choking down water as I tried to time my breaths like the YouTube video I watched the night before. After a few lengths I was hanging onto the wall gasping for air. **Physical appearance was not a predictor of swimming ability.**

But I couldn't quit; there was too much at stake. I'd finish or go down trying. By the time I was halfway through my arms were exhausted and I was choking down so much water I felt like I was going to drown. Every fiber of my being wanted to quit and quelch the pain in my lungs, my arms, and my mind. As I hung on the wall, a strange thought flashed through my mind. If I decided to quit at this moment, when things momentarily got tough, how could I expect to accomplish any of the grand things I envisioned for my life?

I looked at Tim and then the lifeguard, who were both closely watching me—no doubt ready to jump in and save my life if needed. So be it. I was either going to finish this swim test or get pulled out of the water needing cardiopulmonary resuscitation (CPR). Inch by inch I made it from one end of the pool to the other. I finished the test two minutes and forty five seconds over the mark. **I failed catastrophically.**

I had an equally humiliating performance in the treading water portion of the test. I was sorely disappointed in myself and awaited the verdict from Tim like a 3rd grader sitting in the principal's office. "You failed two out of the three tests," Tim told me without trying to soften the reality of my defeat. "Is it possible for me to stay in the class?" I asked. "You can come back one week from now and take the swim test again. If you pass it, then you can stay in the class." This was the deal Tim offered me. I accepted the terms and left the class feeling dejected.

Over the next week, I'd solicit help from a friend that was a lifeguard at Penn State. We met three times at the pool to practice the front crawl and backstroke. I pushed myself to practice, choking down water with each stroke as I struggled to get the timing right. Little by little, I was getting there. Still, getting out of bed to meet my friend at the pool was torture; not a single fiber in my being wanted to get in that water.

I arrived at class a half hour early the following week to retake the swim test. I completed my six laps in nine minutes and fifteen seconds. In one week, I shaved two and a half minutes off my time, but it still wasn't sub 9. "You can stay in the class," Tim said, "but you need to swim six laps in under nine minutes by the end of the semester, or you won't be able to get an A." I would come to learn that Tim was extremely fair and wanted nothing more than for his students to succeed. He'd teach me many lessons in years to come.

When I wasn't struggling for my life physically in the pool, I was fighting for it mentally in Russian. But class was going quite well as I relived my freshman year study habits of spending hours each night with my nose in the books. Strangely enough, I was putting more time and energy into Russian than I was into my aerospace classes. My aerospace professors considered this odd, but I committed myself to learning Russian and I was going to see it through.

The Russian classes at Penn State were in the department of Slavic and Germanic languages. There must have been a few dozen students from the introductory Russian class up through the most advanced. Many students from the College of Liberal Arts took the class to meet general education requirements, a few wanted to be translators, and then there was me: an aerospace engineering student performing near the top of the class. It didn't make much sense at the time to any of us, but it was an exciting new challenge and I was having a blast.

Outside of class we had a Russian club that met every Friday afternoon on campus. The officers brought **пряники** (cookies), **чай** (tea), and **конфетти** (candy). The group included students of all levels, actual Russian speaking international students, and the Russian language professors. We read Russian poetry, watched classic Soviet films, and played board games designed for language practice. It was one of the activities I most looked forward to each week.

As for the aerospace department, classes were moving along just fine. Sal and I had a very similar course schedule since we both took spring semester internships. By this point we became very effective at studying and dividing and conquering all the demands on our time from our classes, extracurricular activities, and social lives. My work with Professor Schmitz was also progressing well. I had a desk next to the Masters and PhD students he advised. I was now learning the research approach to computer modeling in aerospace, which was more detail-oriented than I was used to from classes or internships. I was building models to predict the performance of wings—a fundamental problem in aerospace design and analysis.

My hard work and persistent efforts allowed me to emerge victorious from the fall semester. The undergraduate research I was pursuing with Professor Schmitz helped me secure a slot in a paid research program for the spring semester. This came with a stipend of a few thousand dollars and a more formal research plan, which was exactly what I needed to magnify my focus on that work among my other activities.

In our last meeting of the semester, Sven told me two things. The first was, "Jason, you need to use that money to buy a better computer." I had my original college laptop for several years. And although it was great for everyday tasks, it was entirely too slow to run the engineering models I was building with him. By this point, Sal and I had gotten into something called 'credit card churning,' essentially signing up for credit cards just to get the sign-on bonuses. Although I wouldn't recommend this to people, we were both disciplined and new enough to not let any outstanding debts build up on the cards. I purchased the laptop using another friend's corporate discount and got a powerful engineering laptop with an NVIDIA graphical processing unit (GPU). It was way ahead of its time.

The second thing Sven said to me was much more intriguing than our discussion on computing hardware. "Jason," Sven always started out by saying my name, maybe it's a German thing. "You know this research you've been working on?" he asked. It seemed like a rhetorical question since obviously I knew about the project we'd been working on together for the last four months, but I still played along, "Yes, Dr. Schmitz, what about it?" He proceeded to fill me in, "It's for a space helicopter that we're going to fly on Titan." "Okay, Dr. Schmitz. That sounds cool," I repeated, this time a bit more confused. I wasn't sure what Titan was and I also wasn't sure if Sven lost his marbles.

As it turned out, I had been working on the Titan Dragonfly proposal development team for four months without knowing it. Johns Hopkins University along with Penn State and a few other partners were preparing a NASA proposal for a one-billion-dollar space mission that would send a helicopter to Saturn's largest moon, Titan. There wasn't much online about it yet, so I couldn't even look the project up. It didn't seem like too big a deal at the time, but still, working on a space helicopter for my day job sounded pretty sweet. As time went on, I would find out just how lucky I was to be in the right place at the right time. But the more immediate concern was packing my bags and heading home for Christmas. Another semester complete and just two more to go.

The spring semester came quickly with yet another demanding schedule. I was taking 22 credits, including 4 of Russian and 4 of scientific diving (advanced SCUBA). Without the extra-curriculars, I could have gotten away with 14 credits which would've made for an easy semester. The words of Les Brown echoed through my mind as I contemplated that fact, **"If you do what is easy, your life will be hard. But if you do what is hard, your life will be easy."**

His rhetoric closely paralleled that of my high school physics teacher from four years earlier, "Work hard for the next four years, and the rest of your life will be easy." Well I can tell you one thing—I was certainly working hard. It felt like I was firing on all cylinders and I was somehow still maintaining a social life on top of it all. From Sunday to Thursday, though, I was either in one of my favorite study spots, in class, or sleeping.

The semester was another busy one with another round of large scholarship applications. With each application I wrote, I felt the full weight of my ambitions. It was like a second job—one that would be essential to getting where I wanted to go. I spent every free minute writing the many required essays for all the applications. One of the biggest awards I applied to was the Foreign Language and Area Studies (FLAS) fellowship, which was my ticket to Russia.

FLAS is a year-long scholarship for students studying less commonly taught languages deemed as critical to US national security. Russian was one of those languages—go figure. This scholarship aims to support students obtaining US competency in these critical languages and their respective cultures. These types of fellowships are extremely competitive, but by this point I had learned the skills required to put in a strong application. And I had a great story behind it. My main motivation for studying Russian, after all, was to improve international relations through the space program at NASA. It was an altruistic theme that anyone could resonate with. To make a truly competitive application, I'd have to commit to a semester abroad in Russia. This was already my plan and the timing was perfect as it would round out my fifth year at Penn State (I would already graduate one semester late thanks to my NASA spring semester internship).

Although originally I had my sights set on Moscow State University, arguably the most famous and prestigious university in Russia, my Russian professors swore by the program in St. Petersburg. It didn't make much difference to me as St. Petersburg seemed close enough to the original target, and if the likelihood of me mastering Russian was higher, then that was all the more reason to do it. So I sent in my application proposing two Penn State Russian classes in the fall and a semester abroad in the spring. Then it was time to wait.

Speaking of waiting, I had not heard back on my summer internship application to return to my same group at NASA Ames. I was a bit nervous and decided to reach out to my mentor from the previous spring. It turned out that since I interned at Bell immediately following my time at NASA, they assumed I was no longer interested in working at NASA. The words hit me like a brick. 'No longer interested in working at NASA.' I politely (I hope) reassured my mentor that I was indeed hoping for a return offer. Interning again at NASA, I thought, would allow me to gain more experience as I honed my applications for graduate school. My return to NASA seemed uncertain, but truthfully, there was too much happening to worry about it.

The semester raged on with my demanding course load and extracurricular activities. One of those activities was our wind turbine competition team. We had secured 1st place the year prior thanks to our turbine's advanced technology and a strong business team. The competition alternates each year between a more focused technical one and a larger hybrid competition with business aspects. Mitch and I lost the technical contest two years prior as young sophomores, so this time we were returning with a vengeance.

All year long we'd been working with a small team to improve the turbine's design. I led the aerodynamics team with a handful of folks and set them off in various research directions. It seemed that the way for us to win was to have the most technologically advanced turbine. We spent hours theorizing a new mechanism that would keep all blades operating at their peak efficiency regardless of the wind speed. The technology was ahead of its time and the mathematics and computer modeling required to pull it off was beyond the skill level of our still young undergraduate team.

Mitch continued improving the generator design, essentially an electric motor that the wind turbine drives to produce electricity. We tested multiple combinations of the hand-made generator stages and 3D printed rotor blades.

We had some that were rubbery, some were hard and ductile, while others were brittle. Some were smooth and others were rough. We experimented by trial and error and honed in on the best combination for our turbine.

One of our largest technological leaps was the electronic control system. We'd been chasing something called a buck converter since Mitch and I first got involved in the competition. We estimated that figuring it out would boost our performance by 50-100%.

Advanced skills in electrical and computer engineering would be needed to pull it off. Mitch and I convinced my old freshman summer roommate, Pat, to help us implement the advanced technology. Pat was in his senior year of Electrical Engineering at Penn State and was preparing to jump into a PhD program in theoretical mathematics. If anyone was going to figure this out, it was him. Pat was our secret weapon, the technical ace in our deck.

A handful of us traveled to Boulder, Colorado for the culminating event held at the National Renewable Energy Laboratory. The team was in high spirits having achieved several major advancements in the design since the previous year. We had the best turbine the previous year, and in our testing back at Penn State, we were leaving last year's turbine in the dust.

The team strided into the test room confident and larger than life. We positioned our turbine in the wind tunnel, secured it, and set up all the wiring and electronics. The testing was just about to begin when one of the judges halted the show and pulled out a measuring tape. Our turbine was 3 inches too tall which violated the competition rules. This was no easy fix—the tower that held our turbine was a precision machined part hand made on a lathe back at Penn State. There was no way we could get another one in time to compete by the end of the day. The team was dejected.

We trudged back to our bullpen with the turbine in hand and had ourselves a nice pity party for a good 20 minutes. Some blame was shot around the room in that short period of time as our faculty advisor sat on the sideline to see if we could come together and figure it out as a team. The oversight was our fault and this sort of error has serious repercussions in the real world where we'd also be responsible to fix it ourselves. If we considered the rule on turbine height to be silly, we'd find far stupider constraints in our jobs after graduation. It was an amazing practical learning opportunity for us.

Eventually, the group took a slightly more optimistic tune. We searched for the nearest hardware store—there was a home depot just 20 minutes away. "We have a plan. Will you take us to Home Depot?" we asked our faculty advisor. She obliged- and just like that, the mere action of trying to recover lifted our spirits. We were back in the game.

On the way to Home Depot, we discussed roles and actions so the team could divide and conquer. One of the students was to go find a hacksaw big enough and strong enough to cut our steel tower. Another team member was on the hunt for plumbing fittings to mate the tower pieces back together after a three inch chunk of it was removed. My job was to find J-B Weld—an extremely strong metal-glue-like substance I used on my trips home from college fixing things around the house. In layman's terms, J-B Weld can fix whatever duct tape can't.

We headed out to the parking lot, all of us huddled around the turbine. As soon as we assembled all the pieces back together, we loaded up into the van and raced back to NREL. We arrived just in time for one of the last test slots available. Most of the other teams had already completed their testing and packed up for the day, relieved that the defending champions were removed from the competition.

The team repeated the entire process of mounting the turbine in the tunnel, securing it, connecting and powering up the electronics. It was time to sink or swim. Our Frankenstein tower creaked as it shifted under load with the varying wind gusts. Our once rock solid turbine now looked like it could explode into pieces at any moment.

Miraculously, the turbine survived the hardest part of the testing. **We did it.** The scores were tabulated and awards were presented, the Penn State CWC team swept the board. We took 1st place overall and 1st place in the test turbine competition. It was a picture perfect ending to a long and adventurous journey Mitch and I embarked on two and a half years prior.

We came back to Penn State with our heads held high as we returned our focus to the last days of the semester. Around this time, results from my scholarship applications were trickling in.

The FLAS fellowship office contacted me—I would be funded the following year as one of Penn State's undergraduate fellowship recipients, heavily subsidizing my final semester at Penn State and my semester abroad in St. Petersburg. One very strenuous and action packed year after setting the goal to study in Russia, it looked as if I was on my way. A million questions buzzed through my mind. Which program would I apply to? How would I rent an apartment at Penn State for just one semester? And many more.

There wasn't any time to ponder these questions, though, as you may have guessed by this point in the story. Anastasia gave me a ring on the phone—**I was going back to NASA.**

This semester was one of my hardest as I pushed myself to the limits with coursework, extra-curricular activities, and my new hobbies of Russian and SCUBA. It felt like I was drowning for much of the semester, but all the hard work paid off. And despite how bad it may have seemed at the moment, I made it out the other side. If I blindly followed the advice of others, I probably wouldn't have taken Russian or SCUBA. They were seen as distractions from my studies in aerospace. But those activities pushed me to improve both mentally and physically—they added new dimensions to my personality and my approach to life.

When pursuing your purpose, keep knocking—even if no one sees it for you, and even if it feels like no one will answer. As long as you keep pushing forward, you'll eventually find the door that opens. "Knock and it shall be opened unto you." The quote doesn't say, "Knock and if no one answers, give up and go home." It says, "For every one that asketh receiveth; and he that seeketh findeth; and to him that knocketh it shall be opened." **Just keep knocking—trust me.**

CHALLENGE 8

How We Treat Others

Our interactions with others impact our daily lives in ways we often overlook. While much of how others act is out of our control, how we respond to them is entirely within our power. It's easy to mirror negativity, but it takes strength to respond with kindness and understanding.

Think about a person you've recently had a negative interaction with. Reflect on how you reacted—did you respond in a way that aligned with your best self, or did you let anger or frustration get the better of you? Now, consider how you could approach your next interaction differently. Could you respond with patience, empathy, or even a simple smile? Write down a few ideas for how you can choose a more positive response in the future, regardless of the challenges others might bring. Remember, by choosing to radiate positivity, you're not just helping them—you're helping yourself by maintaining your inner peace and being a force for good in the world.

12. NASA II – THERE ARE ALWAYS FLOWERS

"There are always flowers for those who want to see them."
— Henri Matisse

Throughout my journey, I've faced plenty of ups and downs. Sometimes, the downs are as trivial as a parking ticket; other times, they're as devastating as losing a friend or loved one. If there's one thing I've learned, it's that some things happen no matter what we do. Our reaction to those events is what shapes our day, our week, and even our life.

I remember a close childhood friend whose dad always said, "It's just a thing," whenever something went wrong. Nothing seemed to shake him or get him riled up. Years later, I began to understand the value of his mindset. We can't choose what life throws at us, but we do get to choose how we respond. Looking for the flowers in every situation—the beauty or lesson that's there—helps us see past life's trivial distractions and focus on the bigger picture.

The period between my senior year and my return to NASA was one of the longest breaks I had in years. It was a month filled with several family activities including some time at the beach. I really didn't know how to take 'time-off' at this point in my life. In my mind, not actively progressing was the same as moving backward. So even at the beach I'd have a book with me. I was reading a lot on personal development, finances, and investing. By 'a lot' I mean the time that I spent reading—I was still an atrociously slow reader but could power through a book on vacation.

After a month or so of hanging out with family, I boarded a 6:03 AM flight at the Philadelphia International Airport that would take me to San Jose, California. San Jose is the closest airport to the NASA Ames Research Center where I would be a returning intern for the next 10 weeks. The next adventure was about to begin.

The NASA summer internship program is on an entirely different scale than the fall and spring programs. My organization, the Rotorcraft Aeromechanics Office, was hosting around 40 interns this time around. The group still came from all over the world and we even had a student from Vilnius, Lithuania. Although I had to learn where that was on a map in 10th grade, I absolutely knew nothing about it. We also had several students from the East Coast and a decently sized contingent, interestingly enough, from Kentucky. One of the Kentuckians was Stephen. He was the best violinist I ever heard in my life and would become a close friend throughout the internship.

Returning to NASA for another internship felt different this time. I was more seasoned, more aware of the challenges ahead, yet still excited by the chance to dive deeper into a world of possibility and discovery. I was also becoming skilled in group dynamics; when you throw 30 or 40 people together in a new environment, they very rapidly make assessments of each other as they develop a mental model for the people they'll be interacting with closely over the next few months. I made an effort to learn everyone's name and background in the first day or two and stayed up late in the evening studying the group. Learning everyone's name and studying their interactions helped me find my place in the group. Over time, I'd come to realize that knowing how to navigate these dynamics was just as important as any technical skill I'd develop.

There were two main intern offices, which were big rooms with several cubicle style desk setups. The cubicles didn't have walls all the way around though, just directly behind the computer monitors so you could hang a calendar and not have to stare directly at the person across from you. For the most part though, the room was very open and conducive to interns helping one another and collaborating. The room had about 14 interns, and I sat in the corner with the two other acoustics interns. All three of us were brought in to continue developing the microphone signal processing code I made during my first internship. There was one major tweak though—I was to work on data from a full-scale helicopter test and the other two interns were working on data taken under Mars conditions.

I wouldn't be surprised if you're now wondering why the rotorcraft engineering branch cares about helicopter noise in a Mars environment; that seemed like a pretty odd thing to me at the time as well. The very simple explanation is something called Ingenuity. The first aircraft that was planned to fly on something other than Earth was already heavily under development by the summer of 2017. The little helicopter, weighing just about 4 lbs on Earth and 1.5 lbs on Mars, was hitching a ride to the Red Planet with the NASA Perseverance rover. Ingenuity had a singular overarching mission: to prove flight on another planet possible, which would enhance our capacity for further exploration in the future.

I got the other two interns up to speed with my old code before delicately expressing my interest to Anastasia for working on a different project for the summer. "I know you probably brought me back for me to work with you on acoustics, but I just don't think it's the direction I want to take my career." It felt like I might as well have said, 'acoustics is stupid and I don't like it.' I braced myself as I shared my thoughts with Anastasia, worried she might feel let down. But her response reminded me of the rare mentors who genuinely want to see you follow your passion. "I still want you to finish the acoustics project," she said, "but why don't you start working a bit with the aerodynamics modeling group as well." Despite only being a few years older than me, Anastasia would turn out to be one of the most genuinely caring mentors I've ever come across. So it was settled, I would still work with her, but I'd also dip my toes into computer modeling. I just needed to find a project.

Our first week of the internship was extremely eventful. The parachute that would later deliver Ingenuity to Mars was undergoing testing in one of the wind tunnels at Ames. The 80-by 120-ft. Wind Tunnel was actually the largest in existence. During testing, a portion of the tunnel wall came loose and damaged the facility's motors, which would knock it out of commission for several years. I had my new project: computer modeling of the parachute that would deliver the world's first space helicopter to Mars.

I'd also volunteered in that first week to plan a trip for the entire cohort to go see a SpaceX launch at Vandenberg Air Force Base. It was an opportunity for the group to explore California and spend time with each other outside of the professional work environment. I'd come to find myself in this team building role more and more as time went on.

We combined the trip with a visit to Universal Studios and the California Science Center on the way down. The amusement park was certainly fun, but there's something about a few dozen NASA interns ripping around a science museum that seemed extraordinarily fitting. We got to see the Endeavor space shuttle up close, which was named after the British HMS Endeavor that helped map unchartered territories. In our own way, even as interns, several of us were contributing to projects that would go on to map unchartered territory. It was almost too cool to be real. We continued exploring the science center taking in stunning scenes such as the Apollo 16 command module that brought humans to the moon, and the Mercury program capsule that flew Ham, a chimpanzee, in 1961.

On our way back North, we stopped near Vandenberg to see the SpaceX launch. There were so many spectators that traffic was going to keep us from reaching our intended destination by the time the rocket would take-off. Since the rocket would be visible for miles, we just parked the car on the side of the road and waited. We mostly talked about what we'd seen in LA and the internship experience up to that point.

Since the launch was on the other side of a mountain range, we didn't hear anything for the first few seconds after the count-down timer we were streaming hit zero. Then, as if Thor himself was thundering down upon us, chest-pounding reverberation and crackling from the rocket engines hit us. We saw the Falcon 9 heading skyward at an amazing rate and watched in awe how the engine exhaust plume changed in response to the rocket breaking the sound barrier. To cap off a successful launch, it was SpaceX's first time landing their booster on a drone ship at sea. Elon's vision of reusable rockets was becoming more and more of a reality.

Our summer projects were in full swing by the time we got back to Ames. And later that week, NASA announced its newest class of astronauts. Zena Cardman was among them and she was a SCUBA diving geologist from Penn State University. I took full advantage of being inside the NASA firewall and shot her a quick email. Something along the lines of:

"Dear Zena,

Congratulations on entering the Astronaut program. Wishing you all the very best.

Penn State Forever,
Jason Cornelius"

The signature line comes from one of the PSU football fight songs, which probably only a Penn State undergraduate or someone that regularly attended PSU sporting events would know. Still, it was a lowkey way to say 'Hey! Congrats from a fellow Nittany Lion.' Zena did answer me back, and it was the highlight of my week. It turned out that Tim, my SCUBA diving instructor back at PSU, knew Zena and had worked with her for her SCUBA diving as a Penn State researcher. Small world.

Some combination of being back at NASA, going on our adventure-filled science trip, and hearing the news of Zena getting into the astronaut program had me revved up. I was working long days and making a lot of progress modeling the Mars parachute. My friend Stephen sat directly behind me and we were often the last two in the upstairs intern office. It sometimes felt like we were both waiting for the other to pack up first so we could revel in the achievement of being the hardest worker in the room. At least that's how I felt anyway—maybe he was just working late.

Also across from me was our Lithuanian intern. Having been to China with an entire group of Americans, I could only imagine how difficult it would be to move to a foreign land without knowing a single person upon your arrival. He was good at English, but the abrupt jump into a new culture still had to be challenging along with a new language and a new way of life. I decided to study a bit of Lithuanian, just some simple words and phrases to communicate with him in his native tongue. It was clear to see the excitement in his eyes every time I'd say, 'Labas rytas' (LAH-bahs REE-tahs), which translates to a simple 'Good morning.' I had barely gone out of my way to learn a few simple phrases, and yet it seemed like they had a huge impact on his day. Some of these takeaways were just as important as the technical skills I was learning that summer.

We did still have a few instances of less than ideal cohort dynamics, however, which I suppose is to be expected when you stick a few dozen college students together for several months. One of the most surreal experiences of my life happened when I was staying late at night coding as I usually did. It wasn't unusual for one or two other interns to stick around late as well, but this time Stephen had already packed up and gone home. It was just me and one of the young ladies in the group. She came over and asked me, "How do you do it?"

I think I would've been puzzled even if I wasn't sleep deprived and on my eighth mug of coffee for the day. "How do I do what?" came my somewhat apprehensive reply.

"Why does everyone like you?" she asked point blank. I was cool and confident on the outside, but the question pierced my armor like a dagger. We stared at each other for a few seconds. Despite always having something to say, in this instance, I was speechless. On one hand, her question revealed the very serious and saddening internal struggle she was facing in the cohort that

NASA Pt. 2 – There are Always Flowers

summer, but on the other hand it was starkly contrasted with my own personal growth. I was in her position just over a year earlier on my first NASA internship, and the pain in her voice reverberated through me even more than the rocket had. Before I could say anything, she turned and left the office.

I'd learned to skillfully navigate large complex group dynamics, but it had been a long road with many deliberate steps taken along the way. I didn't know if that was something I could teach someone else, or even if it was appropriate for me to offer. We really weren't close friends up to that point, 'What can I possibly do here?' I asked myself as I sat alone in the office late that night. Work was most definitely done for the day. Her question lingered with me, a reminder of how far I'd come since my first NASA internship, when I'd often had similar questions. It struck me that maybe my growth over these past few years was something she could sense, even if she couldn't envision the outcome she wanted for herself just yet.

I had a stellar schedule that summer. I got up around 5am, jumped on my bicycle, and rode it all the way across Mountain View to the 24 Hour Fitness for a morning workout. I was committed enough to do the several-mile trek in each direction with a workout in the middle before heading into the office. At the time, I didn't think much of what that said about me versus the other interns, it was just the schedule I chose to lay out for myself. Regardless of what it did say about me, the advantage of this early morning schedule was that I had ample time to do things before anyone else was even awake.

A few mornings after my coworker asked me that piercing question, I stopped by a flower shop on my way back from the gym and picked up a dozen red roses. I rode all the way back to the intern housing with them swaying under my handlebars as I pedaled. I took a quick shower and donned my typical attire; it was Suit Monday, which I had gotten a few of the other interns to participate in. But I was on a covert mission and I was racing against the clock. I jumped on my bike again and rode into work, flower bouquet in hand. On the way in, I rode past an intern from a different group that I didn't know too well. I nodded at him and continued on my way.

I put the flowers on her desk and wrote a simple note, "There are always flowers for those who want to see them." Leaving the flowers felt like a small reminder that good can be found anywhere, even in the depths of our own internal struggles. It was my quiet way of saying, 'You belong here, just keep going.'

When she saw the flowers, her face lit up with surprise and happiness. For a moment, the stress of the internship seemed to melt away. It was the best $30 dollars I'd spent in my entire life. There were a few of us in the office by the time she came in, and I got in early enough that no one saw me place them. "Did you see where these came from? Who put them here?" she inquired with an excited note in her voice. "I have no idea." came my dry reply as I stared at my monitor pretending to be working. "Is it your birthday?" I asked, "Sometimes Bill does things like that." She didn't suspect me—I was in the clear and had no intention to tell a soul. Seeing that the flowers had the intended effect was all I needed.

The rest of the internship was filled with more adventures around Mountain View, San Francisco, and LA. Several road trips and weekend activities tightly bonded the group together. On the weekends we stayed in Mountain View, we'd often go gallivanting around Castro Street near Ames. There were nice restaurants and bars with cuisine from all over the world. Castro Street felt almost unreal, like an oasis of vibrant life and culture amidst the work-only mentality of Silicon Valley. These escapes reminded us that excursions outside the office were just as much a part of our experience there.

We'd grab dinner in the evening, then go to one of the bars for a few hours, walk back to NASA, and catch a few hours of sleep before returning the next morning for the farmers' market. I had a go-to route that started out with an iced coffee sold by a Peruvian coffee shop, then I'd make my way over to the Russian stand. There was a nice lady and her husband that sold various Russian breakfast type foods and pastries; it was a great opportunity to practice my Russian, and the snacks were delicious as well.

I wrapped the internship up with a massive report on modeling of the Mars parachute system. My simulations pinpointed the issue that led to the wind tunnel failure. I was intrigued that I could approach a problem, formulate a way to solve it using a computer model, and then systematically work through my hypotheses to a satisfactory conclusion. It was the research process in action, and I was getting more hooked on it each and every day.

On my last day in the office for the summer internship, I made my way down to Bill's office to thank him for the opportunity and say goodbye. Just when I was about to reach his office, however, the young lady with the flowers exited his office and turned the corner. We again found ourselves standing face to face. "It was you, wasn't it?" she asked me with an inquisitive tone. I looked at her and smiled, "I don't know what you're talking about." I was caught slightly off guard by the question now that it was several weeks later. She could read right through me and just said, "thank you" as a slight smile stretched across her face. I turned and walked into Bill's office—I wouldn't tell anyone that story for many years to come.

Later that evening a group of the interns headed to Castro Street for one last hoorah. We stayed out until late in the night and then made our usual walk back to the NASA intern housing as we reminisced on all the experiences we shared throughout the summer. We stayed up a while longer after we made it back before finally retiring for bed.

Around 4 AM that morning I met Stephen out front of the lodge. We had flights departing around the same time and were sharing an Uber to the airport. He was off to Kentucky and I was headed back to Pennsylvania where I'd have my usual one week home before heading to my next adventure. Something felt different about this internship compared to all the ones prior though. It took me until I made it all the way through security, to my gate, onto the plane, and onto the runway for it to really hit me. I'd made some truly amazing friends this summer at NASA. And as the plane started its takeoff roll it dawned on me that I would likely not see most of them ever again.

Maybe the fact that I hadn't slept played a part in it, but all the emotions of the summer hit me like water breaking free from behind a dam. I sat in the front-most seat of my section on the plane, directly across from one of the flight attendant's chairs. Tears welled up in my eyes and started running down my face as the plane ripped down the runway and lifted skyward. The flight attendant across from me could definitely tell; there was no point trying to hide it as the events of the summer flashed through my mind. Challenges, victories, setbacks, friendships, and even some romance were sprinkled in. It was another crazy adventure in the books and I most definitely emerged as a better person thanks to the friends I met and the experiences we shared.

The summer taught me several valuable lessons. Namely how learning a few simple words in someone's native tongue could bring a piece of home to wherever they may find themselves in this huge world. I also learned the joy of a simple act of giving without expecting anything in return. Lastly, in the words of my friend's mother who said it better than me, "People will come and people will go, and that's simply part of life."

Excerpt from Jason's journal, August 15th, 2017:
"My plane ride home was a bit of an emotional time. I've been described as stoic on more than one occasion, so having a good sob isn't very like me. I think it finally all hit me at once that these great friends I made were now scattering all across the country.

Every so often in life we meet people who change the way we view the world. They change how you act, how you dress, and even how you feel. Bill had some moving words on our last day, "Sometimes you'll want to be with somebody and you can't." It's sort of like that. Farmers markets on Sundays, restaurants during the week, going to cafes, getting into mischief at the lodge, and much more.

And although we must head our separate ways, everyone is just a snapchat, call, or flight away. Maybe soon we'll find ourselves crossing paths and becoming close again. As I reflect on the summer, I see how these friendships colored my world in ways I didn't expect. The people I met influenced my actions, thoughts, and dreams—and even though we were parting, the impact they'd left would stay with me."

13. FLYING BY THE SEAT OF YOUR PANTS

"Our deepest fear is not that we are inadequate. Our deepest fear is that we are powerful beyond measure. It is our light, not our darkness that most frightens us."

— Marianne Williamson, *A Return to Love*

Throughout my journey I kept returning to a thought-provoking theory. If we set our mind on something and pursue it with everything we've got, then achieving it is inevitable. I continually tested this theory as I set ever more challenging goals and assembled a record of demonstrated achievement. I surely had my setbacks and failures, but on average, setting audacious goals continuously moved me in a rapid upward direction. Eventually, I would come to truly believe the meaning of this discovery, that "we are powerful beyond measure." And anything we could think or dream of is within reach.

As I entered my final fall semester, the stakes felt higher than ever. Between a grueling course load, applications to top graduate programs, and the pressure to secure funding for my study abroad, I knew I'd be pushing my limits. But if I'd learned anything so far, it was that growth only happens when you step beyond what you think is possible.

I had my typical one week home before reporting back to State College for the fall semester. These weeks at home weren't much of a break as I split time between different sides of the family trying to see everyone. This fall I was moving to a new apartment downtown since I was just going to be there for the fall semester. The location was right in the middle of downtown State College, about two blocks from the fraternity.

My schedule was filled with an intense mix of required aerospace courses and my so-called 'hobby' classes, including SCUBA, Russian, and research. I thrived on the challenge, balancing long days in class with weekend dive trips and late-night study sessions. My 'hobbies' now made up more than half of my schedule and were a full-time courseload by themselves. Looking back on it now—I must have been out of my mind.

Over the summer I was accepted into the study abroad program I applied to at the St. Petersburg State University, which was one of the premier institutions in Russia. The requirements of my FLAS fellowship meant that even the fall semester would have a pretty big focus on Russian with both Russian language and history classes. That was fine by me; I was generally finding them more interesting than some of my aerospace classes, which tended to be dryer and unnecessarily difficult. To explain that a bit further, aerospace classes have homeworks, quizzes, and exams that put you through the wringer. A single homework could take anywhere from a few hours to a few days to complete.

Russian on the other hand was a much more enjoyable challenge. Learning the grammar of how all the words properly fit together was like a puzzle that I didn't even quite know how to approach solving yet. The language is so difficult that textbooks initially simplify many concepts so the student can formulate sentences early on. The further you go down the rabbit hole, however, the more complicated grammar you find lurking beneath the surface.

My daily routine involved waking up before the sun and heading to campus. I'd stay there until late at night. A typical day involved getting up around 6 AM and returning home after 9 PM. On campus I'd bounce between the aerospace building where Sal and I had our aerospace classes, and the Russian building where I took intermediate Russian with the program coordinator. Originally from Moscow, she had an extremely different personality from the professor I had for my first year of Russian. She was tough on her students, but it was certainly tough love. She wanted us all to succeed in our language journey.

My advanced SCUBA course was another challenging one with stark differences from both my Russian and aerospace courses. The class was intended to train students to become certified scientific divers with the American Academy of Underwater Scientists. This was a challenging road to traverse if you actually wanted to become a science diver. The class would step through training for the following certifications: Advanced Open Water, Search and Rescue, Enriched Air Nitrox, and Deep diving.

Pool sessions in the Natatorium were also more demanding, including the initial swim test to get into the class. That's right, every single semester of SCUBA has a swim test to get into the class. The advanced classes upped the ante to a 400-yard swim and 15 minutes of treading water. Luckily I'd become a semi-proficient swimmer by this point, making my way to a pool roughly once per week since starting my SCUBA adventure a year earlier.

This course would take us far outside of the pool though, as we explored the Susquehanna river and several quarries in Pennsylvania. We wasted almost no time and started diving these spots early in the semester. These sites were usually just a day trip, but it certainly was all day. I'd often give up a week-day or a Sunday to go diving. We'd arrive as early as 6 AM at the Natatorium to grab all the gear before hitting the road for our dive spot.

We learned how to conduct scientific research underwater such as recording measurements of the underwater substrate, communicating more complicated ideas to our dive buddies using hand signals, and getting into more advanced diving including the use of dive computers. We also carried additional gear such as oxygen canisters used on longer or deeper dives to prevent us from getting the bends.

I'd also started helping Tim teach the introductory SCUBA course, which was an absolute blast. There were typically three sections per semester, and we had three TA's to cover them. The classes had anywhere from 10-18 students, all with varying levels of water fitness and comfort in the pool. The students took me rather seriously given the atmosphere developed in the class by Tim.

After all, any number of small mistakes could snow-ball to a full-blown emergency on SCUBA. Our job was to give the students enough training and skill to not put themselves in a situation where multiple small errors had a chance to compound into a big one. Teaching SCUBA was an amazing opportunity for me—I found that you only really mastered something when you could teach it effortlessly to others. This discovery would lead me to pursue a number of interesting opportunities in the years to come.

On top of my classes and SCUBA, I was also still supporting the wind turbine team that now won the national title two years in a row. This time around we had grown the team substantially and I was now creating and delegating tasks for several aerospace engineers on the turbine aerodynamics subteam. It had to be that way since I was stretched pretty thin—there really wasn't time for me to be doing much of the engineering. This was my first real glimpse into project management and I found it to be far more difficult than the actual engineering. Formulating complementary tasks, keeping the team motivated, maintaining a schedule—these were all required to develop a successful end product.

These activities kept me very busy, but there was still more to be done. Given that it was my last fall as an undergraduate student, it was time to apply to graduate school programs. It was ironic to be applying after how ridiculous Sal and I thought the idea was in our early days at Penn State. The first step involved taking the GRE, which was the graduate school entrance exam for STEM programs in the US. I did well on the math section which wasn't that big of a surprise, but the larger surprise was that my English competency jumped dramatically. It still wasn't amazing, but all my efforts writing scholarship applications and reading self-help books allowed me to boost my skill-level.

I dwindled the list of universities I would apply to down to five. Penn State where I did my undergraduate studies, two other top helicopter engineering programs, and two more very prestigious engineering programs. All five were in the US. Still, applying to even just five schools was a daunting task. Each had their own requirements, including personal statements, tailored resumes, and long application packages. As if that wasn't enough, I was also preparing my applications for the National Science Foundation Graduate Research Fellowship Program.

The first application deadline was in fact the National Science Foundation Fellowship. I thought back to the stinging words of my good friend who in freshman year laughed at the thought of getting one of these awards, *"only the best students in the world get those."* This sentiment ran through my mind periodically as I pondered the application. The answer was obvious, though, if only I looked within.

It was a 5-year uphill battle that transformed me from that new inexperienced student to a skilled researcher in aerospace engineering. The journey involved well over 10,000 hours of study and work, which is typically the number thrown around to achieve 'mastery' in any one domain. I had no illusions—I had certainly not mastered aerospace, but I felt as if I had a solid grasp on a wide range of the fundamentals.

Still, even with all this success, I didn't know what odds I had. 'Who am I to think I have a chance at something as prestigious and competitive as the NSF Fellowship?' I wondered more than once. Imposter syndrome had me bad this last semester at Penn State. **My resume showed a successful record of achievement, but deep down I was still just a small-town kid from Pennsylvania.**

Excerpt from 'A Return to Love,' by Marianne Williamson:
"Our deepest fear is not that we are inadequate. Our deepest fear is that we are powerful beyond measure. It is our light, not our darkness that most frightens us. We ask ourselves, 'Who am I to be brilliant, gorgeous, talented, fabulous?' Actually, who are you not to be? You are a child of God. Your playing small does not serve the world. There is nothing enlightened about shrinking so that other people won't feel insecure around you. We are all meant to shine, as children do. We were born to make manifest the glory of God that is within us. It's not just in some of us; it's in everyone. And as we let our own light shine, we unconsciously give other people permission to do the same. As we are liberated from our own fear, our presence automatically liberates others."

I heard these words often throughout the semester. They'd play through my mind as I jogged across campus to the Natatorium for my 7 AM SCUBA class. It was the only Penn State class I ever heard of that started before 8 AM, and I trekked all the way up there in the dark frigid cold each week, with the words of Marriane Williamson being read by one of the actors in Coach Carter on some YouTube motivational mashup I'd listen to. I'd sometimes hear them on the way back to the aerospace building all the way across campus, on the way to Russian class, back again to the aerospace building, then to the library, and on my way home again.

Throughout the semester I must have heard those words over two dozen times, which was a good thing because they gave me enough courage to give it a try. I titled my research statement, *"Experimental Characterization of Martian Aerodynamics to Validate a Computational Fluid Dynamics Tool for Future Aircraft Design."* The essay proposed a research plan to further investigate and expand our knowledge of helicopter operation on Mars. My personal statement was a 3-page summary of my Penn State journey.

Excerpts from Jason's NSF Personal Statement:
"**Introduction**: I am deeply committed to the study of our solar system through manned space flight. Whether I am conducting rotorcraft research, leading and mentoring a team, learning a new language, or even obtaining a scientific diver certification, I always maintain this goal on my horizon. Working along the way to push the boundaries of aeronautics, contribute to the advancement of human exploration, and inspire others to pursue their dreams has molded me into the person I am today.

Future Goals and Concluding Statements: Upon completing my undergraduate studies, I will pursue a Ph.D. in helicopter engineering along with a research career at NASA to become a leader in aerospace. Throughout my career I will continue working to change the way the world flies and inspiring those around me to run, perhaps fly, after their dreams. Becoming an NSF GRFP fellow would grant me the freedom to concentrate all my attention on accomplishing these goals, and it is for that reason that I know I would be an exceptional fit for the program."

It was my attempt to manifest the light within me. I spent dozens of hours honing these essays. I solicited feedback from friends, family members, colleagues, and anyone else that would help. There was even a peer-group of students that would read each others' essays and provide feedback. I put everything I had into perfecting them to the best of my ability.

Eventually the day came and it was time to submit my application. It would be many months before I heard one way or the other. As was now typical of my life, however, there was no time to sit around and wait. I had a wind competition team meeting that same day, a Russian exam two days later, and a SCUBA diving trip on the weekend. Not to mention five more graduate school applications to complete.

Things were pretty tough, but I was making consistent steady progress with my 16 hour workdays. That following Monday, however, everything grinded to a halt. A good friend of mine from my time at Bell Helicopter had died. He was a year younger than me and was diagnosed with Stage 4 Leukemia at age 21. Bailey was a great friend that summer and had a contagiously positive attitude towards life. I suppose in some way I had a positive impact on him as well. He handed me an envelope at the intern closing event that I read later that evening; a note that I still have to this day:

Excerpt from Bailey's note, August 2nd, 2016:
"Dear Jason,

This past summer has truly been an awesome experience getting to know and not only be able to call you friend but also a brother. When I say I look up to you as a mentor I truly mean it. You have a level head about everything. you know what you want in life. Above all, what inspires me most about you is your passion. You know you want to work in helicopter aerodynamics for the rest of your life. you have a hot fire burning brightly inside of you and I hope one day I could have a passion that burns just half as bright.

I liked the quote you gave me, but I'm going to leave you with one more: 'Impossible is just a big word thrown around by small men who find it easier to live in the world they've been given than to explore the power they have to change it. Impossible is not a fact. It's an opinion. Impossible is not a declaration. It's a dare. Impossible is potential. Impossible is temporary. Impossible is

nothing.' - *Muhammed Ali.*
         -Bailey"

One year after Bailey wrote me this note, he was pulled off this Earth. It seemed the universe had a twisted way of teaching me life lessons. Bailey's note was a reminder to me that you never really know in the moment how much of an impact you can have on someone's life. Every single person you interact with, no matter if it's the bagger at a grocery store or the barista handing you a cup of coffee, we always have a choice to leave someone in better shape than we found them, to leave a positive mark. It was also one of the first times I truly internalized my own mortality; it pushed me to continuously evaluate how I was living my life. Most of all, I felt a responsibility to follow through on the words he left me. "to explore the power they have to change it." I didn't know what it was that I would try to change just yet. But what I did know—it was a call to action to never settle in life.

I battled for the rest of the semester to keep all the balls I was juggling up in the air. Some of the applications came together smoothly, while others did not. The semester seemed to just keep on punching. In some regards, it was a right of passage to prove to myself what I had become capable of. On the other hand, I wouldn't wish the same experience on anyone. Luckily in January I had a few weeks at home for some much needed relaxation. I had successfully completed all my goals for the semester and emerged mostly unscathed.

I say 'mostly' because I took a beating in my Russian final examination. It was an oral exam and I bombed it to an impressive degree. I suppose with all the balls I was juggling, it shouldn't have been a surprise that I'd drop one of them. Regardless, my professor was upset. She knew I was about to head to Russia and admonished me, "Надеюсь, вы не умрёте (nadeyus', vy ne umryote)." She translated it to English just for good measure, to ensure I got the message given my poor performance on the exam, "I hope you don't die." I was used to professors being hard on me, especially when they knew I could do better. Still, I couldn't help but wonder how much she meant it.

The time at home would be some much needed recuperation and preparation. My next adventure was the study abroad program in St. Petersburg,

Russia. I had received several monumentally helpful scholarships to help fund the trip, including FLAS. Given that a semester study abroad is an extremely costly endeavor, however, I had still come up short on funding the entire trip. I didn't know where I was going to get that extra money. I was considering personal loans with ridiculous interest rates and various other workarounds. Luckily, it seemed life was tired of whooping my butt and would give me a slightly more pleasant lesson this time around.

Excerpt from Jason's journal, December 24th, 2017:

"Well it's Christmas Eve around midnight and I'm laying in bed. Chelsea's been long asleep and my mom and dog are off to bed as well. I don't write in here too often, but something moved me greatly tonight and compelled me to write this before going to sleep.

I was walking to my room when my mom called down the hall, 'There's one gift I want you to open before you go to sleep.' I thought it would be something silly, some Hallmark ornament or something. Instead, I opened it to find a check written out for the amount I'm short for Russia. I looked at it partly stunned, but not too surprised because I knew she would find it somewhere. That's just how she is.

Her giving me the check flipped a switch in my mind that this trip is for real. It would be a once in a lifetime opportunity to truly chase after my destiny. My motivation for what I do comes from many sources, but my mom is definitely a big one. When they say 'know your why' so that when you get knocked down you have a reason to get back up. Well, that's a big part of it for me.

It's odd for me to write the words 'once-in-a-lifetime,' as it feels I've had the good fortune to have many of those throughout my life. This realization does not elude me. On the contrary, it puts an enormous weight on everything I do. The number of people who have gone out of their way to support me on my journey is something I think about often. I feel real responsibility to press forward not just for myself, but for the many people that believed in me at one point or another. Along those lines, I feel that it's my duty to share my experiences and what I've learned with others in the hopes they can also benefit from the opportunities afforded to me.

Related, the students in my middle school teacher's science class had asked her, 'Why do we need to learn all these things?' Her reply probably shocked them—it definitely shocked me. 'We once had a student that learned all this and he made it all the way to NASA.'

I told the story to my grandmother who was another of my childhood heroes. She helped raise me and my siblings while our parents worked full-time jobs. 'Who knows,' she said, 'Maybe you'll go down there and convince a few kids to go into science.' That's when I decided to reach back out to the teacher. I ended up talking to the entire 7th grade class last week, a few hundred students. I may never know the impact I had that day. Still, it was one of my favorite activities of being home this break from school."

14. WINTER TRAINING IN RUSSIA

"Speak to someone in a language they understand, that goes to their head. Speak to them in their native language, that goes to their heart."

— Nelson Mandela

I've learned time and again the power of just a few words in someone's native language. Sure, many people around the world speak English fluently, but which language do they think in? Which language do they use with their family? For those who speak more than one language, their behavior—and even their personality—can shift depending on the language they're using and the context they learned it in.

Despite English's reach, there's something to be gained by speaking to someone in their first language. You unlock parts of them you'd otherwise never see. For me, this was the reason for learning Russian—to become a cultural ambassador of sorts, bridging the gap between our worlds. The end goal? To pave the way for collaboration on the audacious projects of space exploration. Why Russian? Well, there are currently three nations with the capability to launch humans into space: the US, Russia, and China.

I had some experience representing America to the people of China. It might sound funny, but every time we meet new people abroad, we color their view of the states. My goal in Russia was to have this discourse, to have international exchange.

DARE TO DREAM

Excerpt from Jason's journal, February 1st, 2018:

"I'm currently sitting on Аэрофлот (Aeroflot) Flight #38 from Moscow to St. Petersburg. I started my journey yesterday when my mother and I set off for JFK airport. We got hungry along the way so I told the GPS to find a McDonalds, it chose Washington Heights… It was a rough bit of town but I got our cheeseburgers that my grandfather gave me money for. 'Put this in your pocket so you can get a cheeseburger or something on your travels.' It was literally just enough to buy us some cheeseburgers, but I was grateful for every little bit of help I got leading up to this trip. Of course my mom was instrumental in making it possible, but also other family members, neighbors, and friends. It felt like half my hometown pulled together to make this opportunity possible for me.

Breaking through the clouds over Moscow, I saw my first glimpse of Russia—a scene straight out of an old Soviet film, with red-and-white-striped chimneys set against the snow. It felt authentically, unmistakably Russian. The airport had many trucks, plows, and workers, all with ушанка ('ushanka,' a Russian winter hat with flaps covering your ears.) I did pretty well with my Russian on the plane; I even translated for a non-Russian speaker sitting next to me. Border patrol didn't go as smoothly, they searched my backpack but eventually let me in. I'm probably about a half hour from arriving in St. Petersburg where there will be other students and staff waiting. It's shaping up to be quite the adventure.

It's crazy for me to think this is finally here; I worked extremely hard to make it happen. More to come."

I arrived in St. Petersburg, a former capital of Russia, along with the rest of the incoming cohort of American students. For the next four months, we would be engaged in an intensive Russian language immersion program at the St. Petersburg State University. Our first two days in Russia would be spent in the hotel near the airport as we met with the program coordinators, the other students in the group, and some other Russian volunteers.

On the morning of our first day of scheduled activities, I woke up at 4 AM due to either jet lag or the excitement I was feeling. I got up and recorded a quick video for Facebook as I was committed to documenting my experience for folks back home. I wanted to bring Russia to them. I filmed the 39 second video in Russian, reading a script I wrote out on my computer. My Russian was still atrocious, but at least I could construct sentences and convey basic ideas.

We completed our initial introduction and programming at which point our host family's picked us up to take us to our new homes for the next few months. My host father came to meet me. He didn't speak English that well and I didn't speak Russian that well—it was a bit of a rough start. After having some tea, we drove back to the house. It was in one of the best possible locations of St. Petersburg, just a half block South of the Neva River and a half block away from the historical Tauride Garden (Таврический сад).

St. Petersburg was founded by Peter the Great in 1703 as a 'Window to the West.' It was his vision of connecting what would become the Russian Empire with Europe. The city's architecture and layout was inspired by European cities such as Venice, Amsterdam, Paris, Stockholm, and London. Our apartment was on the top floor of a six story apartment building, which was the typical setup for apartments around the city.

There was a bit of a snowstorm going on outside, or at least that's what it seemed like to me. I'd later come to learn that it was just a normal day in St. Pete. When we arrived at the apartment I met my host mother, brother, dog, and cat. I jumped into an entire family. The apartment was stretched out on a single floor. A long hallway had three bedrooms, including mine, branching off of it. At the end of the hallway opposite the front entrance was the living room which wrapped around into the kitchen. The living room was fascinating, it had an entire wall covered with bookshelves and hundreds of books. Even on the other side of the world readers chased me.

Other ornate decorations were sprinkled throughout the apartment. It was evident my host family would have many interesting tales to share if only we could figure out how to communicate. We had a home-cooked meal that night and sat around the dining room table for a few hours talking in a mix of Russian, English, and charades. It was a long day and the next morning would be my first day at the St. Petersburg State University where we'd take our placement exam. After I'd retired to my room for the night, I spent some time gazing out my window. It was hard to believe that just two years after setting the goal to study in Russia, I had finally made it.

Our language program was located in the Smolny Convent (Смольный собор). Smolny was created by Peter the Great for his daughter, Catherine, who would later become Empress of Russia. The university had classrooms all around the city, and I was lucky enough to come to this historic site each day. I lived just a twenty minute walk up the street with a nice stroll past the Tauride Palace (Таврический дворец) along the way.

Another one of the girls in my cohort lived in the apartment just across from mine. We walked to Smolny together on the first day, bundled up to face the harsh Russian winter. Snow fell almost daily in St. Pete; it seemed to hit you in the face no matter which direction you were traveling.

When we made it into the school building, a woman checked our coats. Coat checks were extremely common in Russia and I quickly got used to the idea of it. The ladies working there were polite, but they were sure to tell you if you weren't dressed properly for the Russian winter. On the first day, one of them scolded me for not wearing a proper winter hat. They became like guardians for us. Their reminders to bundle up felt oddly comforting, a motherly gesture in a place that could have felt much colder without them.

We had the placement test on the first day, which was meant to assess our Russian language abilities and split the cohort into four smaller groups that would take classes together. The test was reminiscent of the GREs I'd taken a few months prior: timed, stressful, and leaving you with the feeling that you could have done better.

We received our results the next day; I was placed in the second hardest group. The days were filled with courses such as Russian grammar, phonetics, conversation, literature, and translation. They were taught predominantly in Russian, with English only used as a last resort. We had a crushing amount of homework each night that took hours to get through, probably because it was well beyond my current level of Russian. It wasn't the first time I was in over my head, so I buckled down and trudged forward.

St. Petersburg is geographically located at such a high latitude, less than an hour flight from the arctic circle, that the winter months experience darkness for much more of the day than I was used to. Sunrise was around 10 am and sunset around 5pm. This meant that my walk to school in the morning and my walk back home after classes was done under the veil of darkness, with snow pelting me in the face in each direction.

Classes continued to be extremely challenging. I was fumbling in lecture as I tried to participate in group dialogues that were well beyond my comprehension level. It was a strange feeling—everyone else was successfully communicating, and I just sat there, largely left out. I was butchering the homework and holding back the class. By the end of week one, the program coordinators suggested I might consider moving down a level. It was an embarrassing moment for me, a very public acknowledgement of the situation.

I convinced the coordinators to let me remain in the higher level for one more week. I was used to situations where I'd have to pour it on, and this was no different. I doubled down. I wrote flashcards that I studied on my walk to and from class, my hands chapped from being out of my pockets on the walk. I worked through my homework late into the night with my host parents, trying to grasp the intricate Russian grammar. I spoke as often as possible, writing down any words I didn't recognize to look up later on. Another week flashed by, and I hadn't moved the needle enough.

Here I was taking a semester away from my aerospace studies to learn Russian, and I didn't feel like I was just failing, I felt like I was floundering. I agreed to move down a level, and though it stung, it was the right choice. Being able to follow along in class would give me a fighting chance to absorb—and that is what I sorely needed.

I was now even more determined to come out of the program with a firm grasp of Russian. Although I was in classes from the time the sun came up until it went back down, I knew it still wasn't enough. I needed to get out there and practice it in context. To truly master Russian, I'd need to not only learn the grammar, but to learn the culture and the idiosyncrasies of the language and culture tangled together.

The other American students on the trip mostly hung out with each other, but I made it a point to engage with the Russian program coordinators, building staff, and volunteers. One day in the building cafeteria, which was a small room with seating for maybe twenty or thirty, I recognized some of the Russian student volunteers and asked if I could join them for lunch. They seemed a bit surprised at first, but we then engaged in a fascinating dialogue covering a wide range of topics. These students would become some of my closest friends during my time in Russia.

Excerpt from Jason's journal, February 22nd, 2018:

"Well it sure has been a long time since I last wrote, about 2 weeks. At this moment, I'm laying in my bed with the night light on, Neosporin waiting for my winter chapped hands when I lay down the pen. I almost have so much to say that I don't even know where to begin. I'd like to think I'll remember all the stories and the friends I've made, but that probably is naive. So I'll try to write more often.

What were the main events of the last two weeks? I switched to the next class level down, which was definitely the right choice. I understand a lot more in class now, and I can keep my head above water with the workload. I've actually gotten myself a wee bit sick this week. I haven't been sleeping much since I'm trying to finish part of a scholarship application. Getting up early tomorrow to finish it so I can send it off for review. I still have next week to work on it, which is good and bad. I kinda just want to be done so I can focus on my Russian studies, but we'll see, it would be amazing to get it."

I started developing a great schedule as I settled into living in Russia. I found a gym on Nevsky Avenue (Невский проспект), the main street cutting through the center of St. Pete. The gym was on the top floor of a shopping plaza there, and it reminded me of the gyms I was used to back home. Several benches, free weights, squat racks and more. Just a few months earlier at Penn

State one of my friends asked me, "Yo Cornelius, how come you don't really hit the gym?" My response was quick and clever, "I train my mind every day." This gave my friends a good laugh, as they mostly knew me as the academic chair of our fraternity.

It was a backwards mentality, though. The more I read the biographies of successful people I aspired to be like, the more I internalized that physical fitness was just as critical as mental. I still was getting my fair share of mental snacks as well. I brought a book with me to Russia that was on the 'to-read' list for quite some time, 'Think and Grow Rich' by Napoleon Hill. It was a famous self-help book on the creation of riches. What he meant by riches, in this case, was up to interpretation by each of us.

So my schedule became like something out of a movie training scene when the protagonist is working tirelessly toward a singular end goal. I'd wake up at 5 AM tip-toeing my way through the pitch black hallway into the kitchen to heat up some buckwheat (гречка), which is a Russian breakfast staple. After bundling up from head to toe including long insulated thermal socks, one-to-two pairs of gloves, a hat, a scarf, and one or two jackets, I'd jog the one and a half miles to the gym. I really did more of a slow trot so as to not slip and kill myself alone on the frozen and dark pre-dawn streets. I'd get a quick workout, then walk home to shower before heading to class.

Each day was packed with classes, after-school activities with Russian friends, and dinners at home. After dinner I'd sit at the desk for a few more hours of work as I finished my assignments that were due the next day. Finally, around 10 or 11 PM, I'd lay down and read 'Think and Grow Rich' for a few minutes. The book was dense, it was a mix of self-help, psychology, history, and spiritual manifestation. I still wasn't a big reader, but this book was expanding my horizons. One of the exercises in the book was to list your ideas for creating your better future, whatever your motive may be. On a cold 2018 winter night in Russia, I wrote the letters 'D2D' and drew a circle around them.

Dare to Dream.

Although the initial idea for writing this book came to me during my time in Texas in 2017, the title came to me in my bedroom in Russia, exhausted beyond belief around 11 PM that evening. I'd think about the layout of the book and what story I wanted to tell. 'What would be the name of this chapter?' I wondered about my time in Russia. It started out as simply 'Russia,' but the change to 'Winter Training in Russia' seems to be a much more accurate description of what I felt I was doing there.

Over the next several weeks the group would make expeditions to famous historical sites around St. Petersburg. We'd spend several days exploring the 2.5 million square foot Hermitage, one of the largest and most well known museums in the world. There was more gold in one room than I think most people will ever see in their entire lives.

The baroque era paintings left an indelible mark on me as they intertwined the chaos happening on Earth with a mystical battle up in the heavens—much like my own internal conflicts during that time. The tension between my ambitions and my sense of place often felt like a storm raging both inside and around me. I was directing all my energy into my goal to learn Russian, having set aside aerospace for the time being. I'm sure my trip to Russia, and even my interest in learning the language, was considered a distraction by many of my aerospace professors. For some reason, however, something within me had led me here.

The Russian coat of arms with roots drawing back to the Byzantine Empire, historical artifacts from the prehistoric era, and everything from then up to modern art—it was all there on display. Some of the most interesting pieces to me were those belonging to the Romanov empire.

I was in museums on a weekly basis, where I found solace in modern history as it helped me understand the world we live in today. St. Petersburg had many museums related to World War II, especially the Siege of Leningrad. A time when Nazi Germany laid siege to St. Petersburg for three long years.

Our visit to Piskaryovskoye Memorial Cemetery was one of the most emotionally evocative experiences I've had in my entire life. We saw images of the city during the Siege and how people endured, surviving on meager rations amidst the destruction from aerial attacks. The cemetery was the final resting place for over half a million citizens of the city. The mood was somber as our tour guide read the poem carved in the stone memorial behind us, going line by line first in Russian and then in English. There was strain in her voice as she read the last words. She then turned and walked away, leaving us in quiet contemplation. It was a moving reminder of the horrors of war and the resilience of the human spirit, which thinkers like Aleksandr Solzhenitsyn described so profoundly.

Although a lot of my time in Russia was spent learning about the past, we also had opportunities to celebrate the present and look to the future. One of my favorite experiences from the semester was when my Russian friends took me and a few of the other students to Maslenitsa (Масленица). A massive straw effigy of 'Lady Maslenitsa' is constructed and lit ablaze to signify the burning away of winter. The scene was unique; we saw jousting, ate Russian pancakes (блины 'bliny') with peculiar spreads, saw a little girl getting pulled around on a tire-tube by her father, and even found a goat walking around amidst the festivities. It was a sight to behold—it was Maslenitsa.

I also packed several much more involved adventures into my time in Russia. One opportunity came about mid-way through the program when we had our travel week. Students were encouraged to take a trip anywhere they desired during our spring break from classes. Some students chose other cities in Russia, others Western Europe. My friends proposed a unique idea, "Let's go to Baku."

"Where's that? I've never heard of it," I had to ask. "It's in Azerbaijan," my friends said as they patiently brought me up to speed. "I don't know much about it, but it doesn't really sound like the type of place Americans go as tourists." Their proposition somewhat intimidated me. It was no use, however, the wheel was already in motion. We planned a trip that would take us first to Georgia (the country), then to Azerbaijan before returning to St. Petersburg.

Travel week started with a weekend trip to Moscow with the entire cohort before we'd splinter in all different directions for our individual expeditions. We took an overnight train from St. Petersburg to Moscow, which was much calmer than the overnights I'd taken in China. We arrived in Moscow early in the morning. Our adventures took us to see famous landmarks, museums, and buildings throughout the city. The Kremlin Armoury had a plethora of dazzling Faberge eggs, Russian crown jewels, coronation robes, and chariots. St. Basil's cathedral and the GUM department store were also amazingly picturesque.

None of these historic landmarks, however, were the highlight of my trip to Moscow. Two years earlier at NASA I had set the goal to study in Russia—those two years felt like a lifetime. Back then at NASA, I printed out a picture of the Московский Государственный Университет (Moscow State University) and pinned it above my desk. It was my daily motivation to keep pressing on.

So we took the subway across the city to go see it in person. МГУ (as it's abbreviated in Russian) was built in Stalinist architecture. It blends the look of a modern skyscraper with the Italian baroque architecture that I was already used to from St. Petersburg.

I stood there victorious as I reveled in the scene—a bustling Moscow downtown behind me and the snow-covered МГУ before me. In that one moment, intense feelings of satisfaction welled within me as the challenges, setbacks, and late nights of the last two years flashed through my mind. Learning Russian had been one of the hardest endeavors I'd ever taken on, and I did it while trying to juggle my aerospace curriculum, social and familial relationships, and much more. There were certainly some ups and downs along the way, but in this one moment it seemed like it was all worth it.

We wrapped up our activities in Moscow after a jam packed few days. I enjoyed our visit to the city, but no doubt I was already heavily biased towards St. Petersburg. I headed to the airport with three of my classmates. Our next stop was Tbilisi, Georgia.

We arrived in Tbilisi late at night and the trip started with a bang. We thought we were getting abducted by our taxi driver from the airport. We spoke in rapid, hushed English in hopes that the driver wouldn't be able to understand us. If he pulled into a warehouse, we all agreed, we'd all jump out of the car and fight for our lives. The driver eventually delivered us safely to our AirBNB and we realized we might be in over our heads.

We were all exhausted from the trip but I still pulled out my laptop for a few minutes to check email. I opened one of them and read it to myself, then re-read it twice more to be sure. "Dear Mr. Cornelius, We are pleased to inform you that you have been selected for the National Science Foundation's Graduate Research Fellowship Program." So there I was, in a very foreign land far from home. Thousands of miles away from where my journey had started. I made a decision that night in Tbilisi that would impact the rest of my life—**I would pursue my PhD in aerospace engineering at Penn State.** I went to bed feeling satisfied with the feat I pulled off.

We got an early start the next morning as we only had three days to explore all the city had to offer. Tbilisi is over 1500 years old and its culture certainly reflects that. We toured the city, interacted with its people, and ate its delicious hachapuri and meat skewers which are still today some of my favorite foods in the world.

The highlight of the trip came when we haggled in Russian with a Georgian businessman to have one of his drivers take us three hours to a place called Kazbegi. The driver spoke no Russian at all, but was supposedly instructed to stay with us the whole day and then bring us back safely to Tbilisi. At least we hoped that was the deal we bartered in a shady interaction with this Georgian man in our broken Russian. This time, our driver did randomly pull over on the side of the road. He got out of the car and just left. Our minds wandered for a while wondering what was going to happen to us—a few minutes later he came back with some coffee. We had a laugh and figured that even if we made it out physically unscathed, we might be mentally torn up a bit.

Mount Kazbek is one of the highest peaks in the Caucasus range at a staggering 16,500 feet tall. We weren't there to hike that mountain, though, we were there to see the 14th century Gergeti Trinity Church, which still required a decent hike up to 7,000 ft. From the top, we had the most spectacular view of a snow-capped Mount Kazbek with a layer of fog adding a mystical flare to the scene. I pondered the adventure I was on while I looked across the valley to the mountain range. "Maybe someday I'll climb it," I thought.

We befriended a middle-aged Australian man on the hike. Once back in Tbilisi, which was three hours away, we'd continue to see him multiple times over the next two days. In a city of over a million people, it was nearly a statistical impossibility that we coincidentally bumped into him that many times. He was a bad spy and we knew we were being tailed, but then again maybe they wanted us to know. Despite the several sketchy situations we found ourselves in, whether imagined or real, Georgia was one of the most welcoming places I've ever been to and Tbilisi remains to this day one of my favorite cities in the entire world.

We eventually boarded an evening train for the overnight ride to Baku. We were greeted at the border by the Azerbaijani military, who came onto the train and searched for any sign of Armenian contraband, which was strictly prohibited. The two countries have been in conflict for many years. A man in a black suit eventually boarded our traincar and searched through our bags as we sat there answering his interrogation-like questions. The entire interaction was happening in Russian and at 3 AM.

I assured him that we'd never been to Armenia before, and that we were just taking a few days' travel. Our group was eclectic; we had a Jewish kid from the Bronx, a farm boy from Pennsylvania, a New York cityslicker, and a girl of Latin American heritage. We were supposedly studying Russian in St. Petersburg for four months, yet here we were on an overnight train 2,500 kilometers away. I would have been skeptical, too. The entire ordeal lasted nearly two hours before they finally permitted us into the country. Our nerves were rattled and I must have only slept a few minutes that night, but we made it to Baku.

Baku was another absolutely stunning adventure with its historic 'Old City' having been constructed sometime between the 7th and 12th centuries. The nearby Flame Tower skyscrapers set a contrasting modern backdrop against the Old City's thousand-year old stone buildings.

Despite my thematic storytelling, our trip to Georgia and Azerbaijan was an amazing adventure. It was filled with excitement and a bit of fear, which is often the case when we boldly face what's unknown to us. Interacting with the people of these countries was as much part of my education as was sitting in the classroom studying Russian.

Winter Training in Russia

The semester moved at a blistering pace following our return to St. Petersburg. I had made an extensive social network among the Russian students and was hanging out with them often. We took weekend trips to Pskov, Riga, Helsinki, and Stockholm. Stockholm had long been on my list to visit, as an old friend from my first NASA internship studied there. The Royal Institute of Technology in Sweden (KTH) is Sweden's most famous technical University and has a campus resembling something straight out of Hogwarts.

We also stopped in the Nobel Laureate museum. 'Maybe someday I'll find my name among all these great people who have left a positive mark on the world,' I mused internally. Too scared to share such a thought with my friend. Although I didn't realize it at the time, an internal transformation was taking place during my time in Russia. I was starting to connect the dots in new ways, realizing that the future has many more possible outcomes than I previously could have imagined. My new adventure would just require deciding which of those outcomes to pursue.

As we wrapped up the semester, the last item on the to-do list was retaking the placement exam to quantify our improvement. I was ecstatic to learn that I jumped several spots on the rating scale, the most of anyone in the program. It was a great feeling and gave me satisfaction from my hard and diligent work throughout the semester. I was thankful for the many late nights studying, the 5 AM trots to the gym, the flash-cards I studied while walking or taking the subway, and the many great friends I had to practice with. I faced a very public defeat in the first two weeks, but stuck it out and accomplished my goal to learn the language of the Russian people.

Excerpt from Jason's journal, May 20th, 2018:

"Well the 20th of May is finally here, a day that seemed so far off just a few short months ago. The last two days have been quite sad as I said goodbye to my friends and my host family. I never could have imagined that I would become so close with people from a completely different culture and language.

My last days were filled with walking our dog in the parks, eating hachapuri, having dinner with my host family, and having a final night out on the town with all my Russian friends. Saying bye to the host family this morning was not fun. Tears were shed, but it gave me renewed courage to continue my efforts. An interesting feeling swept over me, because I know they truly 100% believe in me and my dream. I gave them the turtle dove gift from one of my favorite movies 'Home Alone 2: Lost in New York.' The story goes that if you give someone a turtle dove, then you'll be friends forever.

It's been 4 months since I've seen US soil. Seeing the East coast after dropping through the clouds by JFK airport hit me with an overwhelming feeling. It was as if I was coming to this place where I know the possibilities are abundant, but not everyone in the world can access them. Many of my friends from Russia believe they will never make it to the US.

I feel like I understand a lot more than I initially set out to on this journey. The more I learn about the world, the more I feel I can do something to improve it."

My time in Russia was a constant period of reflection as I struggled with my thoughts on the world around me and my place in it. WWII history pushed me to ponder how humans in modern times could become so filled with evil. "What leads one off the path of good onto a path of evil?" I wondered. It wasn't clear that I'd ever uncover the answers to these basic questions, but at least I was developing an awareness of the issues, which seemed pretty enlightening at the time. One of the many motivating factors for me to learn Russian was to enable further technological collaboration in space between the US and Russia. First hand accounts of humanity's darkest hours, however, made me certain that this was the single most important goal I could aspire to fulfill in my career.

I learned an extraordinary amount in Russia as I transformed my thinking from that of a kid to that of an adult. I learned that words in a common language are not always needed to build a friendship, that sometimes the smallest acts of kindness can do more than you'll ever realize, that people rally behind someone with a positive outlook on the world. Above all else, however, what I really learned during my time in Russia was that we are all more similar than we are different. The people I met in Russia, Azerbaijan, Latvia, Sweden, Georgia, Finland, Estonia, they all wanted essentially the same things. They wanted to live a fulfilling life, maybe raise a family, and do some traveling to gain new and unique experiences and perspectives.

Leaving Russia, I felt like I had truly taken control of my destiny. As Henley wrote, 'I am the master of my fate, I am the captain of my soul.' **I came to Russia to master the language, but what I really mastered was myself.** I learned what it meant to build bridges between worlds, finding common ground in the simplest and most human of desires.

Excerpt from Jason's journal, May 20th, 2018:

"This Tuesday (about 36 hours after I get home) I am planning to be at my desk at Penn State. I'll be there six weeks to support Dragonfly, which was selected as NASA's 4th New Frontiers mission, meaning it's actually going to space! Then six weeks at NASA for my third internship. And then, finally, I'll go full speed into my MS fully funded by the National Science Foundation."

15. OATH OF OFFICE

"We set goals not for what we get in accomplishing the goal, we set goals for what we must become to accomplish them."

— Jim Rohn

This quote is one of my favorites. To me, it captures an overarching theme of this book. Some things in life are simply beyond our control. Yet, we still have the power of choice, regardless of the circumstances life hands us. When we truly commit to pursuing a goal, the process of pushing ourselves, stretching, and learning becomes the real reward. Whether or not we achieve the specific goal, we grow through the journey itself. And more often than not, I've found that if we truly give it our all, success will follow.

My 36 hours at home between Russia and Penn State were spent flipping through the more than three thousand pictures I took during my time abroad. I recounted the stories and my experiences to my family as I seemingly evaded the jet lag of moving back across the world. It felt like I was still on that huge wave carrying me from my last adventure right onto the next one.

Some strange things happened as I adjusted back to my American lifestyle. Although I used English every so often in Russia, by the end of the trip I was predominantly speaking in Russian. As I told stories, I'd have momentary lapses where I wanted to say an easy word, spoon for example, but the Russian equivalent (ложка) was slamming against the front of my brain trying to come out. My mom would get furious with me; she couldn't fathom how one forgot English. I also had to re-learn smiling at strangers. In Russian culture, it's a bit weird and creepy to smile at strangers you walk past on the street. This was another unforeseen adjustment I had to consciously work to revert back to the American way.

I eventually made it to Penn State where I'd conduct research for the summer as I waited for my St. Petersburg classes to make their way to my Penn State transcript for graduation. I had already planned to split the summer six weeks at Penn state and six weeks at NASA where I'd return for my third internship later that summer.

The first few weeks at Penn State involved diving back into Dragonfly, where I'd be ramping up for a significant design effort over the coming months. I'd go from working on the project part-time to a full-time graduate researcher. With the announcement a few months earlier of Dragonfly's selection as the 4th New Frontiers mission, the team was rapidly expanding in both numbers and scope.

Now that the mission was green for go, Sven and I started diligently working on an improved helicopter blade design. The summer was packed as I sat in on meetings where we discussed aerodynamics, power systems, orbital trajectories, atmospheric entry, parachute technology, and much more. I was operating at full-steam and was having a blast. As one of the early members of the team, I was able to see how all the parts of this massive one-billion dollar space mission fit together. I also observed team dynamics and saw from the very top to the very bottom of the organizational hierarchy. The interconnectedness of the various groups made it feel more like a startup at times.

I had a desk in one of the graduate student offices in the aerospace building at Penn State. Hammond, one of the oldest buildings on campus, has recently been replaced by a state-of-the-art engineering complex. Still, for several years of my life I made almost daily visits to Hammond. This summer was so busy that even on Saturdays and Sundays I found myself there in the office.

Hammond was directly across from a place called Cafe 210. It was a bar, but my labmates and I used it as more of a lunch spot. State College was pleasant in the summer, which was a nice break from the harsh winter ahead of us. One day I went over to Cafe to grab food with some of my labmates as we often did. This time, however, was a bit different. I got a phone call midway through eating—I recognized the area code as Moffett Field, California. **It was NASA.**

I picked up the phone and discovered Bill on the other end. "Hey Jason! Do you have a minute to talk?" Bill asked in the same energetic manner I was used to. It was a nice hot summer day as I stepped out of the Cafe patio onto the College Avenue sidewalk so I could hear him a bit better. Bill went on, "We'd like to offer you a position in the Pathways program, if you're still available and interested." He had a funny way of stating things. A few months earlier I had applied to the NASA Pathways internship program, which allows you to convert from a NASA intern to a full-time NASA employee. "That would be a real honor," I replied. "I would be ecstatic to do that." When I hung up our short phone call, I had a decade-long dream within reach.

There was only one thing left before I could officially consider myself a real NASA employee—the United States Oath of Office. In the US, civilian government positions are still considered federal jobs. And as such, we're required to take the specific agency's Oath of Office to officially become a federal employee.

I finished out my six weeks at Penn State and made the cross-country trek back to Silicon Valley, CA. Since I was only there a few short weeks, I found a temporary setup in the next town over. I'd ride my bicycle through the cool California morning air to the local railway transit line. From there, a 15 minute journey snaked around the tip of the Bay to the Southern access point of Moffett Field. I'd hop back on my bicycle and ride the rest of the way into the office. The long commute meant that many nights I'd find myself crashing on Stephen's floor, who was staying in the intern lodge again this summer. Especially if I left work late enough to miss the train home.

I arrived mid-way through the summer internship after the rest of the interns had already been working together for several weeks. They had already established their circles of friends and some semblance of a dominance hierarchy. Although I came in late, I was a 3rd time returning intern, which marked me as someone that knew what was going on around the office and to a lesser extent, the broader NASA environment.

The fast pace of work at Penn State carried directly into my time at NASA. One of the senior members in the office, and my mentor for the summer, was one of the earliest advocates that postulated helicopter exploration on Mars. He helped enable the public, and NASA, to be mentally ready for programs such as Ingenuity and Dragonfly. His preferred technical term was 'Planetary Aerial Vehicles.' What this really means is space helicopters.

I worked closely throughout the summer with both my NASA mentor and Sven as I built computer models to simulate Dragonfly flying on Titan. In addition to my work, though, the intern group was primed to have a lot of fun throughout the summer. Another one of the students had parents coming from the Soviet Union—one was from modern day Ukraine, and the other from Russia. She spoke Russian fluently and we practiced it almost daily.

Bill thought it was neat that we could communicate in Russian. One day he joked with me, "Okay so you've learned Russian, big deal. Now it's time to learn Mandarin." I chuckled in the moment, not realizing then the seriousness behind his statement. The weeks at NASA seemed to peel off the calendar as I had daily meetings with folks on the East coast working on various parts of Dragonfly.

I poorly attempted to balance the demands of the project with our intern adventures and the social dynamics I engaged in within the group. It was apparent, to me at least, that I was fumbling the ball. Although I was making some progress, I was most definitely not working to my fullest potential and found myself rather distracted. I wondered at times if being a third time returning intern with the full-time position waiting for me had made me too comfortable. "Have I started to settle on my laurels?" came an unsure voice only heard deep within my own mind. "Do I really deserve to be here?"

I wouldn't have time to search for answers to these questions just yet, though that would surely come in due time. Consistent with the rest of my story, the wave was ready to take me from the previous adventure onto the next one. The day had finally arrived for us to officially enter the NASA Pathways program.

That morning, I took the United States Oath of Office and became a Civil Servant at NASA. It was the culminating moment of chasing a 10 year dream.

I, Jason Kyle Cornelius, do solemnly swear that I will support and defend the Constitution of the United States against all enemies, foreign and domestic; that I will bear true faith and allegiance to the same; that I take this obligation freely, without any mental reservation or purpose of evasion; and that I will well and faithfully discharge the duties of the office on which I am about to enter. So help me God.

I did it. I am a NASA aerospace engineer.

Excerpt from the Prologue:

So this is where I found myself in summer 2018. I was floating on top of the world and felt like I was unstoppable, for a brief moment of time.

But then Penn State gave me a phone call, "You are not allowed to both work at NASA and be sponsored by the National Science Foundation for graduate school." The words shocked my system as my dream began to crumble around me. A million thoughts flashed through my mind as I walked down to Bill's office. He'd been working at NASA for more than 40 years and immediately could sense the seriousness of the situation. "Come on in, sit down," he suggested.

The NSF fellowship sponsoring my graduate school was three years long. "Worst case scenario," Bill said, "we'll see each other again in three years' time." His reassurance helped me calm down, though the uncertainty lingered. We would just have to wait and see how things unfolded.

CHALLENGE 9

Your Mission Statement

Taking NASA's Oath of Office marked the culmination of a 10-year journey for me. It also created a framework for me to operate under. Write a personal mission statement for your life, career, or specific goal. Include your core values and how you plan to uphold them. This step is immensely important, as achieving your goal won't be worth anything if you did it acting in opposition to your values. The world has enough bad in it; be a force for good.

REFLECTIONS

"If we're being honest with ourselves, the most interesting question we can ask, and search for an answer to, is Who. Am. I." — Unknown

I would like to close this out with a few thoughts and perspectives that I've developed throughout my journey. I hope some of them resonate with you, and if they do, that they can help you to push towards whatever it is that you choose to demand out of life.

Dreams and Aspirations
"Twenty years from now you will be more disappointed by the things that you didn't do than by the ones you did do. So throw off the bowlines. Sail away from the safe harbor. Catch the trade winds in your sails. Explore. Dream. Discover." — Mark Twain

I decided to become an aerospace engineer and work for NASA at twelve years old. The ensuing journey to achieve that goal would take me on what has truthfully been the adventure of a lifetime.

There's a quote on this theme that I really like, "Live full, die empty." Looking back on my journey, the impetus that led to all my crazy escapades and experiences was my dream to work at NASA and my child-like will to ignore the common belief of what was possible for me. Throughout this story I've chronicled a number of my greatest adventures, some of my highest highs, and lowest lows. It had its ups and downs, and there were many times that I wondered if it was all worth it. 'Was I sacrificing too much?'

I now spend a considerable amount of time pondering philosophical questions about life and our role in it. Oftentimes I think about what it means to live a fulfilling life. I can honestly say I feel as if I have lived one or two lives already even at my young age. I've successfully achieved a number of my goals, while I failed at some others. The fun in setting big goals is not strictly in attaining them, rather it's in the adventure required to pursue them.

DeltaV

In the first year of aerospace engineering we study a concept called deltaV. When a rocket launches to space, some parts of the rocket are shed as it climbs higher and gains momentum. These boosters as we call them are along for just a phase of the journey and help the rocket blast skyward, fighting against Earth's gravitational pull.

Similarly, sometimes the people and experiences we encounter in our lives are just like the boosters of a rocket—they help us fight against the vicissitudes of life until we have built up enough momentum to continue skyward on our journey. Just as the rocket can't reach space without those boosters, we often can't reach our highest potential without those people and sometimes even parts of ourselves that were only meant to be along for part of the journey. And while it may feel like a loss when they fall away, it's often their contribution that allows us to soar.

The Unknown

"And if you gaze long enough into an abyss, the abyss will gaze back into you." — Nietzsche

Ending a chapter of our own life story should never be seen as a loss. Instead, it's a sign that a new one is about to begin—a chapter brimming with new challenges, experiences, and opportunities. And if we're fortunate, it will bring us new friends and companions who will challenge our perspective on the universe and our place within it.

I've met many people throughout my journey that were scared to go after their dreams for fear of what others might think, fear of failure, or even worse—fear of success.

Maybe they would discover something about the world or about themselves that they think would be too much to handle, feelings of doubt, insecurity, rejection. I've had these fears as well, but every time I go into the unknown, I come out the other side having learned valuable lessons that make me a better individual. I don't always succeed, but I can promise you one thing: if you don't try, you fail by default.

Launching into the unknown can be intimidating, just like Nietzsche's words on staring into the abyss. Most of my proudest achievements, however, were on the other side of fear.

Truth

"The truth will set you free" is a mantra we've all heard at some point. It's said so casually that we almost miss the magnitude of its meaning. I've had the good fortune to not run into too many snakes in the garden along my journey. But when I do, it's always evident what one sacrifices to behave in a dishonest way. We all learn right from wrong at a young age.

There are opportunities throughout our lives, however, where we must choose between the truth and some alternative. I've found that choosing anything other than the truth has a much deeper negative impact on our lives that we could even begin to imagine. Sometimes the truth hurts, sometimes it yields short term discomfort or difficulty, but living an outward story different from our internal dialogue creates dissonance within the mind that the body must work to reconcile. It demerits our own credibility to ourselves. So if you're at a fork in the road and you must decide, choose the truth. That will almost always lead you in the right direction.

You are the Foreman, the Director, and the Leading Actor

I heard an interesting story recently about how each morning when we wake up, one of two foremen arrives in our mind. Our brain is more complex and powerful than we can even begin to imagine. It has the ability to reason, to think, to create, to feel. Our mind receives inputs from our surroundings all day every day, and it's our mental attitude that shapes how we respond to them.

Foreman number one comes into the factory of our mind and says, "Alright everybody, the boss isn't feeling too great today. He's got a bit of a cough, a stack of work on the desk, and is behind on his bills and his dreams. Why don't you all just go back home. We're not working today."

In an alternate universe, however, foreman number two arrives on scene in a clean pressed suit. "Listen up, everybody! Can I please have your ATTEN-

TION. The boss said we're having a great day today and we've got a lot to do. There's a pile of work on the desk to blast through, we've gotta get out and make some money, and we need to make some progress on those goals he set last week. Let's go people, everybody hustle!"

The story makes it sound a bit silly, but this is exactly how we can approach each and every day. We cannot always control what the world hands us, but we most certainly can control how we respond. Be careful which foreman you choose to run the factory of your mind.

Wield the Pen
"Believe you can, and you're halfway there." — Theodore Roosevelt

I finished the remainder of my third NASA summer internship and headed back to Penn State for graduation. I then immediately jumped into a rigorous Masters degree program with a full course load and a full-time job on Dragonfly. The following months and years would prove to yield many more challenges, opportunities, setbacks, and victories. Far more than I could have imagined. That story, however, is still being written. On my current journey, there are countless times when I have choices in front of me.

Do I choose the beaten path or the road less traveled? The adventure or the safe haven? We all have decisions that shape the future of our lives. When I realized that we wield the pen to our own life story, things became much more interesting for me. Today, I honestly believe that humans can achieve anything they put their minds to, no matter how ridiculous it may seem to others. Even when someone tells me something absolutely crazy by the standards of popular opinion, I can't help but wonder if they'll actually pull it off. We each have the ability to write our own life story, so pick up your pen and write a good one.

Be a Roger Bannister for Others

Time and time again I saw the role that educators play in how someone's life works out. I owe much of my success to people like Mr. Garraoui and a handful of others who helped me envision what my life could be like. My highschool classmates were right—I didn't know anyone who worked for NASA. But as my story proves, that's not a good reason to not try.

My older sister Chelsea ended up becoming an elementary school teacher, and to this day has positively impacted hundreds (if not thousands) of kids' lives for the better. Although I chose a slightly different path, it's been clear to me, at least looking backwards, the times that I've been able to positively impact someone's journey. The note from Bailey is a constant reminder to me that someone may be looking up to you without you even fully realizing. So be the mentor and role model that others need you to be. They need you. The world needs you.

Enjoy the Journey

"Life moves pretty fast. If you don't stop and look around once in a while, you could miss it." — Ferris Bueller's Day Off

One of my reviewers for this book commented on balance, postulating that not all things must be 'for the resume' or 'for our careers.' I came to this conclusion myself later in life, as my story suggests, but my friend is absolutely spot on. And although I work so hard because I love what I do, I also realize that we never know just how much time we have left. I still think it's okay to go all in on something and really devote your heart and soul to it (this is one of the best ways to ensure success in my opinion). But nowadays I make it a point to enjoy the little things that make life so meaningful.

CHALLENGE 10

Your Future Self

Write a letter to your future self, imagining where you want to be in five or ten years. Include words of encouragement, lessons from your past, and a reminder of why you're pursuing your goals. Stick this letter away, whether leaving it in this book on your bookshelf, or somewhere else that you'll be able to find it. Come back to it whenever you need some inspiration. And remember, regardless of what happens, we do not set goals for their attainment. We set goals for what we must become to achieve them. Imagine not just where you want to be, but also who you want to become.

EPILOGUE

It was four years after receiving that phone call from Penn State before I was permitted to return to NASA. I made it back to Ames in 2022 for full-time work. The journey from 2018 to now (2024) was a tumultuous path with victories, setbacks, and some of my worst defeats yet. Along the way, I discovered a lot about myself and my true motivations in life. I met friends the world over, some that would be by my side for a long time, and some that were just there for a season to share unique experiences with me or teach me a valuable lesson. Lessons of friendship, lessons of love and loss, lessons of putting others before yourself, and lessons of just how valuable this life really is.

My journey has definitely become even more of an adventure after my return to NASA. I've had my breath taken away, been awe-inspired by the smallest things, and had my perspectives changed by the shortest and most seemingly trivial encounters. As it turned out, I would discover soon after arriving back to NASA that my journey was just getting started. That story, however, is for another day. It is still being written.

What lies ahead in the next few months, well I guess we'll all just have to wait and see. But don't worry, I'll make sure it's a story worth hearing about.

Wishing you much success,

Jason K. Cornelius

Dr. Jason K. Cornelius

TREADMILL PROMPTS

Thought-provoking questions and prompts about themes in the book extended to life.

1. What was your biggest failure in life? What was your biggest success?

2. What would you do if you knew you couldn't fail?

3. If you could have a conversation with your younger self, what advice would you give?

4. If time and money were no objects, what passion would you pursue?

5. What moments in your life have made you feel most alive?

6. If you could ask the universe one question and get a definitive answer, what would you ask?

7. What legacy do you want to leave?

8. What are the invisible forces that shape your decisions (society, family expectations, personal fears)?

9. There are three pills you can choose from: one to give you all the money you'd ever need, another to see someone again that has passed away, and another to cure an ailment that plagues people on Earth. Which one would you choose?

10. What does it mean to live a meaningful life?

11. "It's the soul afraid of dying that never learns to live." What are your fears holding you back from?

NOTES

NOTES

NOTES

NOTES

NOTES

NOTES

ABOUT THE AUTHOR

Dr. Jason Cornelius grew up in the small town of Mountain Top, Pennsylvania, where his dream of becoming an aerospace engineer felt as distant as the stars. But Jason never gave up. Today, he works as an aerospace engineer in Silicon Valley, California. He earned his PhD from The Pennsylvania State University, where he contributed to the design of NASA's Titan Dragonfly lander. Jason continues to support Dragonfly, pioneer advanced Mars aircraft designs, and develop cutting-edge AI and machine learning methods.

This book shares Jason's journey from a mischievous small-town kid to an aerospace engineer, pilot, and polyglot, tackling challenges at the frontiers of space exploration. His story takes readers around the world—from China to Russia to NASA and beyond—showing how perseverance and determination can turn even the biggest dreams into reality.

Jason is passionate about fostering innovation in aerospace and inspiring others to dream big. His next adventure involves building great teams to tackle the world's toughest engineering challenges and pushing the boundaries of what's possible.

STAY IN TOUCH

Thank you for sticking with me all the way to the end. It means so much that you've shared in this journey. If you enjoyed this book or found it meaningful, I'd love to hear from you. A review on Amazon or Goodreads not only helps spread the word but also lets me know what resonated with you.

If you have feedback or ideas for how I could improve in future projects, I'd welcome your thoughts. Let's keep the conversation going!

Feeling inspired? Share a summary of your challenges, reflections, or goals on LinkedIn, Instagram, Facebook, or anywhere you connect. Don't forget to tag me so I can celebrate your wins with you! Want to take your journey to the next level? Join the Dare to Dream Skool community to engage with others aiming skyward.

Instagram: @jason.k.cornelius
LinkedIn: @jason-k-cornelius
Skool Community: skool.com/daretodream
My Website: jasoncornelius.com

www.ingramcontent.com/pod-product-compliance
Lightning Source LLC
Chambersburg PA
CBHW021156160426
43194CB00007B/761